THE TOP TEN

1 2 3 4 5
6 7 8 9 10

1

F E R R

S A L U T E T O

First published in 1991 by
Top Ten Publishing Corporation,
42 Digital Drive, Suite 5,
Novato, California 94949, USA

THE TOP TEN

Printed and bound in
Hong Kong.

The information contained in
this publication is correct to the
best of our knowledge. Both
author and publisher, however,
disclaim any liability incurred as
a result of its use. The publisher
acknowledges that certain words
and model designations are
the property of Ferrari Esercizio
Fabbriche Automobili e Corse
SpA. This book is not an official
publication.

ISBN 1-879301-00-8

About Criteria, Patina and Making Lists...

Putting together lists seems to be a popular thing to do. Everyone and everything, from the worst dressed on New York's social scene, to the best wines of California's Napa Valley, get their classification.

The automotive enthusiast is certainly no stranger to the idea. From more or less serious show judging to the auto magazines' annual issues of the best new cars, the ultimate is always being sought and defined.

The criteria for making lists span a spectrum from whimsical to absurd. But since there has to be a discipline to the process, one would certainly not make a list without criteria.

These are some thoughts on the guidelines used in the Top Ten selection process:

Style and engineering. The forms that combine to create the look of a car are important. The machinery that makes it perform is important. But the two can not function separately. They are equally important.

History. A model earns its spot in automotive history based on the qualities defined above. These aspects determine its place in the production history of the manufacturer as well.

Then there is the search for the factor that sends a particular car to the front row. It can be racing history. Or it can be the first of the breed. Or the last. It can be an original owner whose life and personality adds the shades of nostalgia.

Condition. The ultimate is for an old car to still be in a state of like-new condition. But this is, depending on the era, virtually impossible to find. The teeth of time never cease to chew away at the perfection of paint and rubber and leather. At best, on rare occasions, this deterioration process can create the super-ultimate: a car that blends new and old—a car with patina.

Two levels down from the super-ultimate—one notch down from the ultimate—comes the perfectly restored machine, the one that has been executed with respect for history and its unique requirements—which vary from car to car—and not only to the exacting demands of the often cold and sterile need for making new.

In the end, there is no perfect list. One generated by a panel of objective experts often becomes as controversial as one put together by the single, subjective individual.

So here it is, our list of The Top Ten Ferrari Spyders. Thanks to Enzo Ferrari and the men he inspired, it is a selection studded with stars, regardless of how one looks at it. Enjoy!

CONTENTS

The Top Ten

7 PAGE 86
250 California

This topless Ferrari has lived two lives. In its youth: racing at Le Mans. In retirement: luxury in the lap of a European resort. Photographed in the Swiss Alps. Owner: Paul Pappalardo, Fort Lauderdale, Florida.

10 PAGE 116
365 Daytona

First of the last of the real spyder Ferraris, this is the prototype. And the owner didn't even know it until recently. A restoration put it back the way it was when first shown in 1969. Owner: Andrew Cohen, Beverly Hills.

8 PAGE 96
365 California

The forgotten Ferrari—the factory didn't even print a brochure! This luxurious survivor was once owned by the family of feared Dominican strongman, Trujillo. Owner: Robert Beecham, London.

6 PAGE 74
250 Testa Rossa

This super performer for Ferrari privateers never set a tire on the race track. All authentic, it is the Virgin. Ran at a screaming 7000 rpm for the camera on the tip of Long Island, New York. Owner: Anonymous.

9 PAGE 106
275 NART

A wildcat Ferrari that turned out to be a winner: a movie-star, a magazine feature, and a race car—Sebring saw it circle the track all twelve hours to capture second in class. Owner: Dano Davis, Jacksonville, Florida.

Salute to the Spyder

The true Ferrari spyder is a rare breed. How really rare I did not realize until I began the research for this book, when I found that of the ten models finally considered for The Top Ten selection, a total of only 204 units had been built.

Considering the implications, it is mind-boggling to ponder the enormous impact these few have had on the world of car enthusiasts; I am tempted—at risk of conjuring too grandiose a scale—to paraphrase the famous words by Winston Churchill: *Seldom have so few meant so much to so many.*

Of course, if the scope of the selection is widened to include the rare Pinin Farina Spyder and the long-wheelbase California Spyder, as well as the 275 GTS, 330 GTS and the 365 GTS, the production numbers change dramatically, adding another nearly 400 units.

And if the *false* spyders, the targa Dinos and 308s, were also figured in, thousands would be added—but then, certainly, we would be playing an altogether different ball game.

With this introduction, I have already defined the scope of the book. For my final selection, I narrowed it down to only the true spyders—in other words, not targa top models—and of the true spyders, only the absolute

cream of the crop—as it must be in any top ten selection.

But before we go any further, the question of what a spyder is—historically speaking—should be addressed.

The word *spyder* is a term with its origins in the turn-of-the-century coachbuilding trade, where it was used to describe a small, light, horse-drawn wagon for two occupants, suited for fast driving. In order to be light, it had to be constructed in the most weight-saving way, using slender components, and thus looked like a spider.

The word has a Dutch ring to it, and it is entirely possible that the term was first used in that country. As used in Italy, the spelling can be either *spyder* or *spider*. As far as I know, Ferrari did not deploy the term as an official designation until printed in the first Spyder California brochure, and then spelled—as we have seen—with a *y*. By the way, both Fiat and Lancia used the *spider* spelling.

Next, we must take a closer look at the main categories of cars—based on their purpose—produced by Ferrari.

The first group consists of the grand prix cars, which do not fit the spyder definition—although small and light—due to their typical single-seat configuration.

The photographs on these pages show the successful blending of style and engineering--aspects that must interact ideally in order for an automobile to attain its ultimate purpose. Above, a close-up of the hood of King Leopold's 375 Plus Speciale, with that barren black surface broken only by the arch of the air scoop and the rectangle of the Prancing Horse badge. To the left, the Ferrari badge comes up for closer scrutiny, as mounted on the hood of a Spyder California. On the opposite page, a photograph showing the essence of a classic Ferrari spyder at speed--a 166 MM in this case--an image shattered by vibrating, primitive power.

INTRODUCTION

From a study of factory build sheets, it can be learned that Ferrari often used Spyder Competitione to describe his topless sports racing cars...

On this spread, drivers' views of classic Ferrari spyders. The images span three decades; the old print to the right shows the dash of an early 166 Barchetta Lusso, with its plain, leather covered dash and cowling. Below, the sophisticated style of King Leopold's cabriolet and, on the opposite page, the neat gathering of gauges of a Testa Rossa. At the bottom of this page, the dash of the Daytona, which added speedometer and clock.

The next group consists of the sports racing cars, which splits into two sub-groups: the closed, or *berlinetta* versions, and the open, or *spyder* versions. Both, according to the rule book, had to have two seats. In their topless form, these cars therefore fit the spyder definition.

From a study of early factory build sheets, it can be learned that Ferrari often used the term *Spyder Competitione* to describe his sports racers. Based on this, it would have been perfectly logical to have thrown these cars into the selection pot—although I chose not to do so, featuring instead particular cars that, even though they were clearly built for racing, sported an individual history of road use.

The reason for this, although the spyder theme to my thinking calls for road use—going back to the vision of the two occupants in that little turn-of-the-century contraption—is that the dividing line between road and racing cars in the early days was nearly nonexistent.

There was in fact a time—well illustrated by the Barchetta–when the only difference between a competiton car (called a Corsa) and a road car (a Lusso) was that the latter sported leather on dash and cowling.

It used to be that road cars were detuned for their less

taxing task. With the Spyder California, all this changed and the track version had to be given special treatment to fit the role of competitive racer.

This leads to the third group of Ferrari machines, the road cars, of which the majority were berlinettas. Certainly the topless variations qualify as spyders, athough the cars featured roll-up windows, a feature certainly unknown to the spyder concept. This was one of the early signs of the great Ferrari going soft, giving in to the demands of a market where the take could be more substantial.

Half of the Top Ten selection falls into this category. In three of the cases, Ferrari employed the spyder term as designation: the 250 California, 275 GTS and 365 GTS. This was another devaluation of the term, one that would lead to its improper use on the present-day targas.

Two further aspects entered into the selection process. First, in order to facilitate the inclusion of the most attractive models, I opted to stay within the classic era of coachbuilding— not classic in the sense of Isotta Fraschini and Lancia, but in the sense of Ferrari—which spans the fifties and sixties.

Secondly, I wanted to stay in the front-engined, sixty-degree

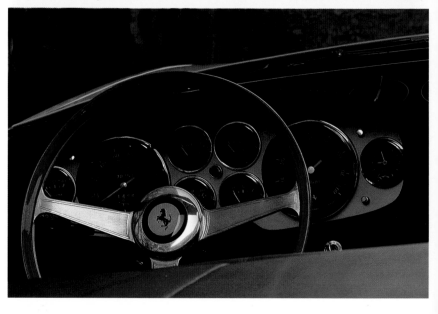

With Pinin Farina's spyder body, the machine became the epitome of power and beauty, all an expression of an era when sports cars embodied pure animal qualities...

The animal characteristics that inspired the classic Ferrari style are poignantly illustrated by these headlights--aglow like the eyes of beasts. Opposite page, top, the voluptuous visage of the Testa Rossa. Below it, left, the shark-like countenance of a 375 Mille Miglia and, to the right, the drawn-out, flounder-flat expression of a 365 California. The image at the bottom of this page, of Michelotti's Mexico, asserts a forward-striving motion better than most.

V-12 era, which, coincidentally, reaches across into the same period of time.

Thirdly, I wished there to be a fair representation of cars covering the entire period, which of course excluded some that a micro-purist might have liked to see. Perhaps, in a more biased selection, all would have come from the fifties.

A question some may ask: Was it possible to select a Top One? The answer is yes. The 375 Mille Miglia.

Fellow Ferrari scribe, Dean Batchelor, writes about a 375 in his excellent book: Ferrari, *The Early Spyders and Competition Roadsters*. With his permission, I repeat his observations.

My first recollection of the real performance of these cars was from a position alongside the Pan American Highway in 1953, about 20 miles from the Carrera finish at the Juarez airport. We had driven ahead of the field before the start of the last leg, on the last day of the race. The road was now closed to traffic and we, along with thousands of native spectators, awaited the racing cars.

Finally, off in the distance one could hear the unmistakable sound of a V-12. It had to be a Ferrari, but which one? All of a sudden Maglioli's 375 MM machine shot the crest of a hump in the road, suspension almost at its lower limits, but the wheels not quite airborne, squatting to the upper suspension limits as the car settled back down and not so much as the slightest lift of Maglioli's throttle foot. As he passed us at full bore in fourth gear (probably around 170 mph), the exhaust dumping into the vacuum behind the fast-moving car made an absolutely shattering noise.

We were interested in his lead over the field, so we started our stop watch and, by actual count, we could hear the Ferrari being down-shifted for slower bends, and then back up through the gearbox to fourth on the straights for a full five minutes. Admittedly, wind conditions were just right.

This is the kind of memory and the kind of writing that this machine inspired.

When it was later dressed in Pinin Farina's spyder clothing, the car rose to a peak of power and beauty, a perfect expression of an era when the sports cars embodied pure animal qualities. See if you don't agree.

Henry Rasmussen,
San Francisco, March 1991

1949

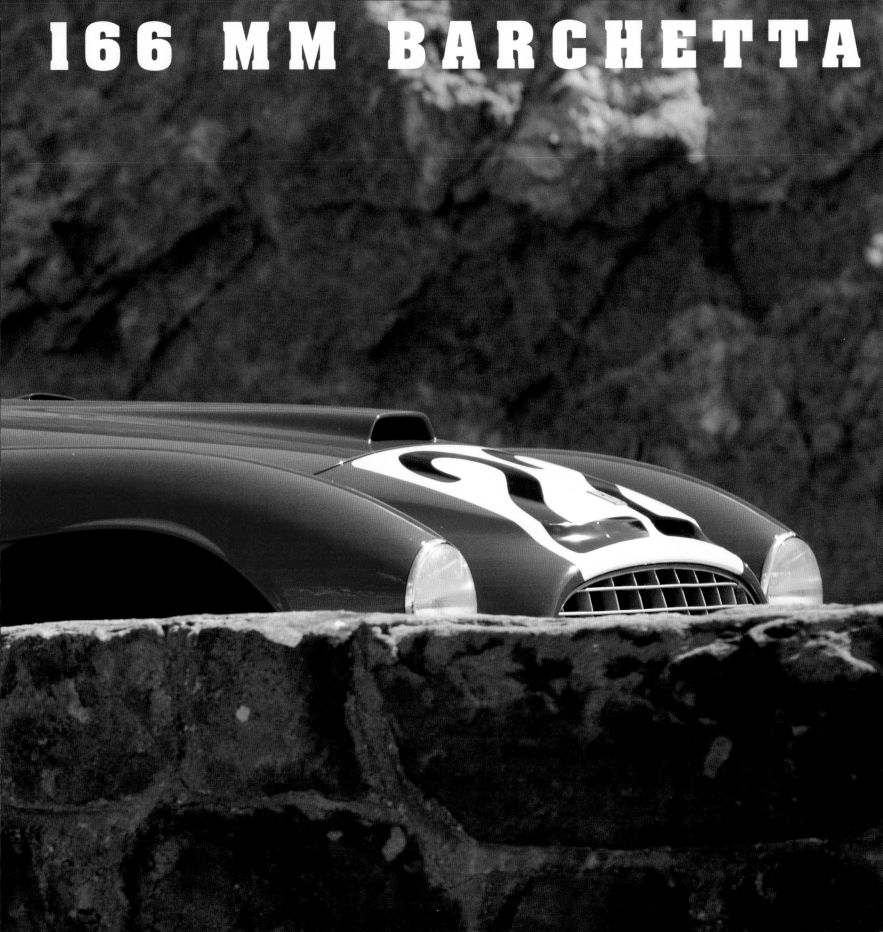

First of the Ferrari World Beaters

During the late fall of 1945, at a time when Italy was still struggling to free itself from the shackles of war, the most essential part of Enzo Ferrari's great master plan for dominance of the world racing scene was already taking shape, although at this point it was visible only as geometric figures, executed on rough sheets of ordinary wrapping paper.

Finalized in the unassuming surroundings of a small Milan apartment, the set of drawings defined the design of Ferrari's first engine—the progenitor of that fabulous generation of V-12 classics—and represented the absolute essence of knowledge accumulated by the legendary Gioachino Colombo, whose brilliant mind had spawned Alfa Romeo's all-conquering prewar Tipo 158 race cars.

Early in 1946, Ferrari retained another Alfa veteran, Giuseppe Busso, to fill a post as director of the technical department, and charged him with responsibility for the operation that eventually transformed Colombo's static shapes and figures into a living and breathing machine.

Late in the year, Busso was joined in this choice assignment by another brilliant engineer, Aurelio Lampredi, whose name, perhaps more than any other, has become associated with the development of classic Ferrari racing power plants.

On September 26, 1946, the piercing, high-pitched voice of Ferrari's firstborn was finally heard throughout the halls of the factory. Then, in March of 1947, the engine was mated to the chassis and taken out for a test run along the open roads around Maranello.

On May 11, the Tipo 125, as the primordial Ferrari would be christened, stood ready for its baptism, an event scheduled for the Piacenza Circuit. Piloted by former Ferrari errand boy turned racing driver, Franco Cortese, and with Enzo himself attending, the equipage led convincingly until, regrettably, the fuel pump quit with one lap to go.

The first Ferrari victory was secured two weeks later when Cortese, competing on the Caracalla Circuit near Rome, managed to beat back a strong challenge from Nando Righetti and his Stanguellini.

During the remainder of the season, further successes were recorded, primarily as a result of contesting a great number of regional events. But the ultimate glory, that of a win in Italy's most famous endurance race, the Mille Miglia, eluded Ferrari when his lone contender, again piloted by the untiring Cortese,

Shades of yesterday are visible in the pictures on these pages. To the left, top of the page, Luigi Chinetti guides 0008 through the legendary Esses during the 1949 Le Mans. The illustration is copied directly from the front cover of one of those day's most popular racing magazines; color photography as well as color printing techniques were in the throes of birth and rebirth, and so was the postwar racing scene--that year's Le Mans, was the first since 1939.

Recaptured below, chassis 0008--one of the all-time most significant Ferrari survivors--as it appears today, once more displaying the same number it did during those memorable twenty-four hours. Present owner, Bob Baker, dons his classic helmet and goggles for this recreation of nostalgia. Chinetti--as he looked a dozen years ago--is seen on the previous page. The wily veteran became one of the great driving forces behind Ferrari's success.

Recalling the shape of a small boat, the little Barchetta expressed a distinctive beauty that was born of a functional need...

did not make it to the finish line. It became evident that without further development, the Ferrari, in spite of its numerous strong points, would amount to nothing more than a local success.

The 1497 cc Tipo 125 was therefore expanded to 1902 cc, which caused power to jump from 72 hp to 125 hp. The initial emergence of this significantly fortified machine, called Tipo 159, came at Pescara in August, where Cortese took a second. Raymond Sommer put a period to the season—and the racing career of the 159—with a win at Turin's Valentino Circuit.

For the 1948 racing season, Colombo's V-12 experienced yet another enlargement, and now sported a volume of 1995 cc, or 166 cc per cylinder. Thus was born the Tipo 166, the car that would become Ferrari's first *World Beater*.

The 166, with 140 hp under the hood, revealed its mettle by winning the grueling season-opening Giro di Sicilia. In the Mille Miglia, next event on the calender, the Prancing Horse was represented by four private entries in addition to the lone 166 entered by Scuderia Ferrari. Piloted by Clemente Biondetti, the latter succeeded in holding its own against a strong field of Alfas, Cisitalias and Maseratis,

giving the Commendatore his first major success.

With the Tipo 166, Ferrari commenced the practice of supporting his racing activities through the marketing of cars to the public—a public which at this early stage was represented by a few independently wealthy gentlemen drivers.

The 166 S (Sport) and the 166 I (Inter), of which a combined grand total of 39 cars emerged, represented the first examples of this policy and were stamped with odd serial numbers. Since these cars were primarily meant for road use, special attention was paid to comfort.

The 166 MM (Mille Miglia), which was developed exclusively for racing, was stamped with even numbers. Almost every one of the 33 units built saw some form of racing action. Six of the cars were owned and raced by Scuderia Ferrari and, as such, acquired countless battle scars before being sold.

All except five of the cars in the First Series 166 MM (units completed between late 1948 and early 1951) sported spyder bodywork by Touring. With their smooth contours and intimate cockpits—recalling the shape of a type of speedboat commonly seen on Venetian canals—the cars expressed a unique beauty

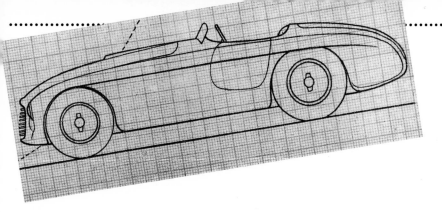

The timeless beauty of the Barchetta grew from the fertile mind of Carlo Anderloni, the creative force behind venerable Carrozzeria Touring. Seen to the left, a fading copy of the original side-view drawing as used in a 1949 Ferrari advertisement. Opposite page, the frontal view of the little Barchetta, first exposed sports car enthusiasts to the grille that would become classic. Below, Chinetti's Le Mans mount as it looks forty years later.

The illustration at the bottom of the opposite page, shows the Barchetta frame mated to the light Superleggera body structure. The example shown is chassis 0068. Seen on this page, to the left, the first Barchetta, chassis 0002, introduced at the Turin Salon on September 15, 1948. As the story goes, it was purchased off the floor by Los Angeles playboy Tommy Lee, who never raced the car. Note the out-of-character whitewall tires. The machine still survives, unrestored, hidden in a Los Angeles collection.

With the 166, Ferrari commenced the practice of supporting his racing activities through the sales of cars to the public...

born of a functional need. The fans approved, christening it the *Barchetta,* or *Little Boat.*

Carrozzeria Touring rose to primacy during the twenties, propelled by the trend-setting designs it generated for the Alfa Romeos of the day.

In the thirties, the company continued its front running pace by inventing the Superleggera system, a method by which a skin of aluminum was stretched across a light superstructure of slender steel tubes.

After the war the firm, now headed by Carlo Felice Bianchi Anderloni—who had taken over after his father's death in 1948— kept producing forms that tied in nicely with the past.

When Enzo Ferrari went to Touring for the design of the 166, the firm responded with a new form, one that proved to be as significant an interpretation of the spyder as the firm's prewar Alfas had been.

Beneath that beautiful body hid a 2200 mm wheelbase frame built from oval-section steel tubes—electrically welded— its stiffness ensured thanks to a mid-section X-brace. While the basic design was executed by Colombo and, as with the engine, refined by Busso and Lampredi, the initial few frames were not built in-house but by Milan-based Gilco.

The front suspension featured double wishbones and transverse leaf springs. The rear featured a rigid axle, semi-elliptic springs, and a stabilizer bar. Houdaille shock absorbers were handling the damping chores.

The wheels were fifteen-inch Borrani center-lock wires, which provided ample brake cooling as well as a view of the huge aluminum brake drums.

The gearbox was mounted in unit with the engine. Fourth gear was direct while, unusual for the time, a fifth gear provided an overdrive option. Synchromesh was available only between third and fourth gears.

The Colombo motor featured a sixty-degree vee-angle, had two valves per cylinder, and one overhead camshaft per bank. Siluminum alloy was used for the block, while the pistons were of cast iron. The cylinder heads were also of Siluminum, and reflected the usual high level of workmanship characterizing Ferrari's own foundry.

The 166 MM featured a 10 to 1 compression ratio. Breathing was administered through a trio of twin-choke 32 DCF Webers, units that were made exclusively for Ferrari (the initials stood for *Doppio Corpo Ferrari*). Maximum power output came at 6600

The color photos on this spread, show the no-nonsense innards of Ferrari's 1949 Le Mans winner. The engine was different from other 166s, in that it sported needle bearings. The fuel tank came from the Grand Prix cars, and held twenty-six gallons. The black and white photos, for comparison, show the 166 MM driven by Dorino Serafini in the 1950 Silverstone Daily Express Production Car Race. Note the single-carburetor setup.

This car and its pilot, Luigi Chinetti, can take credit for the exploit of being the first to place the Prancing Horse on the world map...

rpm, while top speed, contingent on rear axle ratio, arrived near the 135 mph mark.

Turning our attention to the Top Ten selection, the choice is simple and obvious, namely the car with the most outstanding racing heritage. In this respect, no other example can compete with the one that won the first postwar Le Mans in 1949, serial number 0008.

The car and its pilot, wily Luigi Chinetti, can take the credit for the historic feat of being the first to place the Prancing Horse on the world map.

This magnificent Barchetta, then, captures the Top Ten spot and, as it appears on these pages, also represents the first of the spyders saluted.

When Chinetti steered 0008 across the finish line, the event marked his third win at Le Mans. The first came in 1932, the second in 1934—both behind the wheel of Alfa Romeos.

Born in 1903, Chinetti had a love affair with fast machinery already from the start, joining the Italian Air Force at the age of thirteen, only to be kicked out when his actual age was soon discovered.

Chinetti's next stop was Alfa Romeo in Milan, where the young racing enthusiast became an engineering apprentice. He stayed with the firm for many years and eventually made the acquaintance of Ferrari, head of Alfa's racing team.

The thirties found Chinetti living in Paris as the Alfa agent. In 1940, with Hitler's armies closing in on the city, Chinetti traveled to Indianapolis with the Harry Schell team and when Paris fell was unable to go back. In America, he managed to find work as an experimental engineer for the Navy.

After the war, Enzo invited him to Maranello but Luigi soon elected to return to Paris, where he established himself as the Ferrari distributor.

Chinetti bought his Le Mans mount from Ferrari for $17,000. The car must thus be judged a private entry. The sum was split on a forty-to-sixty basis with Lord Selsdon, a wealthy British racing enthusiast.

Chinetti drove all through the night. By morning he had gained a three-lap lead. It was his intention to remain in charge behind the wheel during the complete twenty-four-hour battle, but the officials prevented him from doing so, demanding that his co-driver, Lord Selsdon, take over. The Englishman agreed reluctantly. His stint, lasting only three laps, set the car back an

The illustrations on this spread focus on the cockpit area of the Barchetta, a habitat both decoratively intimate and primitively purposeful--qualities that define the true spyder. No speedometer was needed--the driver went by the tachometer. The Le Mans winner is a Corsa (competition) model. A Lusso (luxury) version, sported leather on the dash and cowling--an environment depicted in the black and white photo to the immediate left.

Chinetti drove through the night. It was his intention to remain behind the wheel for the duration of the twenty-four-hour battle...

Chinetti entering the S-bend soon after the start, foll[...] photograph shows the earth banks which m[...]

Ferrari W

entire lap. With Chinetti back in the driver's seat, the machine again circled the track as steady as a clock, screaming past the pits approximately twelve times per hour, which translated to an average speed of about 90 mph. Then trouble began.

First, it was a minor problem, the driving light, set right in the middle of the grille. It refused to stay on. Regulations required its presence, and a stop on the track as well as one in the pits corrected the defect.

Then, a most serious problem reared its ugly head: the clutch began to slip. Step by step, lap by lap, the situation worsened. The seal had broken, and nothing could be done. Drenched in oil, Chinetti could only watch the competition tear into his lead like hungry wolves. But he kept his cool, finishing the race with a nine-mile margin.

It was a glorious moment for the forty-six-year-old Chinetti, the veteran of so many Le Mans battles, and for the three-year-old Prancing Horse, whose first Le Mans outing it was.

After its grueling ordeal at Le Mans, chassis 0008 lived a much easier life. For a number of years the survivor belonged to a succession of Swiss owners, who raced it in lesser events. In 1968 it traveled to America

and Ed Bond, who a year later sold it to Carl Bross, who in turn shipped it back to Europe and Anthony Bamford, the British enthusiast, who gave it the first complete restoration.

Another transatlantic journey transferred the car to Tom Price. He, in turn, sent it to Italy, where Dino Cognolato, the Vigonza-based craftsman, performed the second restoration.

Today, the old workhorse has found a home with Bob Baker who, to his credit, does not treat the equipage as the priceless museum piece it is, but rather as the potent racer it was.

Baker drove it in the 1989 Mille Miglia, finishing the race on one bank of cylinders. In the Monterey Historic, Baker spun a bearing. After a whole year of recuperation in Phil Riley's Corte Madera, California, shop, where the car was tended to by David McCarthy, the machine was back to perfect running condition and ready for a Top Ten photo session.

A fast drive along the Pacific Ocean, with foggy air flowing across the minimal wind screens and rapid firing rapping on the eardrums, convinced this writer that the Barchetta was indeed one of the absolute highlights of an era when machines were brutal, and the men who drove them were brave.

euillet (Delage) and Savoye with a pre-war British Singer. The robably the safest road circuit in Europe for spectators.

1949

at Le Mans

The yellowing clipping from the July 1, 1949, issue of the venerable British magazine Autocar, bridges the distance in time between now and then. The old photograph shows Chinetti and his 0008 Barchetta passing the packed grandstands on his way to victory. The photograph below, recreates the dusky quality of Le Mans--blazing headlights, Mulsanne fog and all. The present owner welcomes every possibility to exercise the old workhorse.

1951

Forerunner of the Ferrari Style

As much as *Ingegnere* Ferrari might have wanted them to be, the cars he fathered were definitely not just machines. They were certainly creatures of style as well.

Efforts to settle degrees of importance, however, would of course be futile. How can one decide on a line of demarcation that dispassionately separates form from function? The two go hand in hand.

Ferrari certainly realized the value of wrapping his product in a beautiful package. Proof of this is found in the fact that he, in selecting stylists, always knew how to choose the best.

By the same token, the men he selected for this honor seem to have responded in kind, as if energized by the far-reaching possibilities of the machinery. It is no coincidence that some of the most outstanding creations in the field of automotive styling came to grace Ferraris.

The Barchetta, and the studio responsible for its styling, illustrious Carrozzeria Touring, unquestionably staked out the path for the look that, down the road, came to emerge as the classic Ferrari style.

As much as the styling of the Barchetta turned out to be the beginning, however, it proved to be the end as well, for Touring

did not progress along the path it had established. The reason for this seems to have been that the fiscal end of the equation required a shift to the production of the longer runs provided by Alfa Romeo, and away from those short runs done for Ferrari. The task begun by Anderloni and his talented staff at Touring was therefore perpetuated by Vignale and his stylist of choice, a young Michelotti.

But even this formidable team was only an interim caretaker of the Ferrari style. In the end, it was Pinin Farina who brought the theme to its ultimate maturity. The cooperation between him and Ferrari was consummated in 1952, when Pinin Farina joined the board of the Maranello firm as one of its directors.

The logical step, then, in our search for a Top Ten choice, was to bridge the gap between Touring and Pinin Farina—to find that one quintessential Vignale-bodied Ferrari.

The Vignale/Michelotti team began its work for Ferrari in a rather tentative way, creating a series of orthodox bodies. By 1951, however, the two had hit their stride, manifested by fresh new styling efforts. Among these, a series of six cars stood out, soon emerging as a forerunner of the Ferrari style.

Avant garde Italian movie director Roberto Rossellini, was an automotive enthusiast of the first order. A loyal customer of Ferrari's, he purchased not only the first topless Ferrari, but also the beautiful machine featured here. It was a present for his actress wife, Ingrid Bergman. Pictured above, the controversial couple is seen reviewing a script. To the left, the scene is less serene, with a tearful Bergman begging her husband to drop out of the 1953 Mille Miglia, a race that as usual was marred by a number of serious crashes. At the top of the opposite page, the Michelotti sketch that guided Vignale in his work on our Top Ten choice.

Michelotti's design was as perfect and unadulterated as a rock in a mountain pass, sanded smooth by the constant wind...

The simple, flawless lines of the Rossellini/Bergman 212 Export, can be viewed in the large color photo below. Alfredo Vignale--a portion of his business letterhead is shown on the opposite page--was responsible for the manufacture of this body. A panel-beater since the age of eleven, his experienced eye and unfaltering hands produced some of the most stunning cars of the late forties and early fifties. He died in 1969.

While the Barchetta created its effect through the introduction of a number of quite superficial elements, such as creases and folds, this new Michelotti design was perfectly clean, as smooth and unadulterated as a rock in a mountain pass, sanded smooth by constant wind.

Two other Michelotti features gave the Ferrari style a further push forward. The first was the lowering of the nose. The second was the re-angling of the grille, which he slanted inwards at the lower end. Both measures set the stage for the introduction of a pointed nose.

Of these six cars, four were berlinettas, leaving two spyders. Chassis 0090 was purchased by Umberto Marzotto, one of the prominent racing brothers. This was the second of the spyders, built in March of 1951.

The first, chassis 0076, turned out to have been the property of another famous Ferrari patron, Italian movie director Roberto Rossellini, who in fact bought the little spyder for his actress wife, Ingrid Bergman.

Roberto Rossellini made his debut on international movie screens with the World War II epic *Open City,* a film that was first released in 1946.

In 1949, flush with American dollars from Howard Hughes and his RKO Pictures—windfall from a deal that called for the filming of *Stromboli* with Ingrid Bergman—Rossellini purchased a 166 S, chassis 011, sporting a Cisitalia-inspired cabriolet body by Stabilimenti Farina. This was the first topless road machine produced by Ferrari.

Later purchases by Rossellini included 0235 EL, which was a Pinin Farina convertible, and 0265, a Pinin Farina coupe. In total, Rossellini is believed to have owned at least half a dozen Ferraris, which makes him one of the most prominent supporters of the young firm.

With the most fascinating among automobiles embodying not only a machine and a style, but also the history of a man and his passion—qualities that must be part of a comprehensive selection strategy—the Marzotto and the Rossellini cars were certainly equal. In the end, the edge was given to the latter, being the first built.

During filming on the tiny Italian island of Stromboli, Rossellini and Bergman, who were both married, soon became romantically involved. When the gossip could no longer be suppressed, the set was invaded by the press, whose steamy accounts elevated the affair into a full-blown scandal.

The Rossellini/Bergman 212 made its debut at the 1951 Turin Salon. The photograph to the right, is believed to have been taken during that event. At this point in time, Ferrari engaged the services of a number of coach builders--a Stabilimenti Farina sign is reflected in the dark Vignale body, while the light car behind it sports a Superleggera Touring badge. Seen on the previous page, a three-quarter rear view of Vignale's 212. The lines inspired a following.

Through it all, Rossellini never lost his love for fast cars, and he in fact competed in the 1953 Mille Miglia...

Nearly forty years of wear and tear have been surprisingly kind to the Rossellini/Bergman car. Its badges are still the original ones, with that of the coach builder--found on the lower area of the side panels, just behind the front wheel well--seen in the photo below. Further down, a close-up of the Ferrari badge, its Prancing Horse as animated as ever, in spite of the signs of aging--nothing can beat the nostalgia produced by fine patina.

A son was born to the couple just prior to the release of the film, which did not sit well with the public, nor with the critics. Bergman was effectively banned from Hollywood, and spent the next few years making a number of films with Rossellini, whom she married in 1950.

It was a stormy relationship, both on and off the set, and their creative cooperation did not work out. Through it all, Rossellini never lost his love for fast cars, and he in fact drove in the 1953 Mille Miglia.

A number of serious accidents marred the race, and a tearful Bergman managed to persuade her husband to drop out.

Our Top Ten choice illustrates the Tipo 212 configuration, which represents the logical step up from the Tipo 195. This car in turn hailed from the Tipo 166. Power for the 195 was 135 hp, while the 212, with its 2562 cc capacity, was credited with an even 150 hp.

These figures vary, however, often depending on the number of carburetors fitted. In the case of the Rosselini/Bergman car, which features a trio of Webers, the performance factor is said to be around 170 hp.

The Colombo engine had by now passed through a number of development stages. These, in the hallowed tradition, were prompted by lessons learned on the race track. The Colombo design had been based on the assumption that supercharging would be employed. When this approach was ruled out, the siamesed intake porting proved limiting, and with the Tipo 166 arrived a revised intake layout, with six ports—a design that improved breathing.

The primary development, however, was in the incremental increase of the volume. This was, to begin with, attained by lengthening the stroke. From the 166 on, however, the stroke was set at the enduring figure of 58.8 mm. Future alterations, producing the 195 and the 212, were accomplished through an increase of the bore.

Chassiswise, our 212 feature car is virtually identical to its Tipo 166 ancestor, although the wheelbase saw an increase by 50 mm, to 2250 mm.

Otherwise, the front and rear suspensions stayed the same. So did the five-speed gearbox, with its direct-drive fourth and geared-up fifth.

The Ferrari factory, which is known to have exaggerated weight claims, gives a figure of 1765 pounds for the little Tipo 212—perhaps a bit too optimistic even for a car featuring an all-aluminum body.

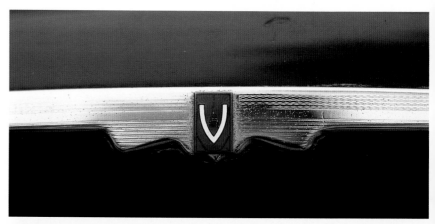

Ferrari 212 Export
Spécial pour
Miss Ingrid Bergman
Carrozzerie de
Alfredo Vignale

It was mainly in the design of the front section, that Michelotti's creation set a direction for the next phase in the continuous evolution of the Ferrari style. The young designer with the futuristic ideas, lowered the nose portion, and angled the grille back at the bottom, thus producing a fast, forward-moving image. The photograph above depicts a sign--in spite of its French presumably shown with the car at the Turin Salon--spelling out its star connection.

The clouded faces of the gauges, the soft dullness of the aging aluminum, the sun-bleached yellow of the badges, weave strong strings of nostalgia...

Although not one of Ferrari's most brilliant performers, the Tipo 212 earned an honorable entry into the record annals thanks to its victory in the 1951 Carrera Panamericana.

Rossellini and Bergman went their separate directions in 1955, when she left for Paris to work with the French film maker Jean Renoir, but not before her husband had given Pinin Farina the assignment to build another car for her. This was the futuristic 375 MM of 1954, featuring a scope-like rear end design and covered headlights.

Nothing is known about our Rossellini/Bergman car while in their possession—not whether he used to race it, nor whether she ever drove it.

Also unknown, unfortunately, are the details surrounding its first sale. What is sure, however, is that by the early sixties the 212 Export had indeed been exported, as it now surfaced in Salt Point, New York.

In 1966, the car appeared in an ad placed by Webster Todd, then of Princeton, New Jersey. No asking price was listed, but the ad stated that $6,000 had been invested.

In addition to the purchase price, this sum had bought a restoration that left twenty-eight coats of red lacquer (the car

is thought to have originally been black) atop those sensuous hand-hammered surfaces.

Today, 0076 is in the hands of a collector who prefers to remain anonymous. It seems the car has hardly been touched since the superficial restoration of twenty-five years ago.

The present owner agonizes over whether to leave the survivor suspended in a state of historic limbo, or give it a state-of-the-art restoration job.

It is certainly becoming more and more rare to see a Ferrari of such an early vintage as this, still in virtually original shape. Somehow, the clouded faces of the gauges, the patina of the worn leather, the dullness of the aging aluminum, the bleached yellow of the badges, all create strings of nostalgia—ties to the past—and all would be severed by a restoration.

On the road, the old machine is riotous—loud, rough, primitive, and potent. It is not any quicker when it comes to top speed than its predecessors, but the torque is magnificently magnified, its curve remaining strong between 3000 and 5000 rpm, and still creating the sort of acceleration that is felt in the spine all the way up to 100 mph.

Restored or not, the car will remain a milestone—a forerunner of the Ferrari style.

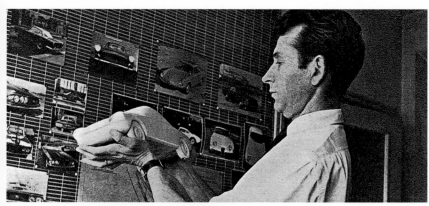

An old-world craftsman, seen in the photograph to the far left, practicing his trade at the Vignale shops in Turin. To the near left, Giovanni Michelotti, photographed in his studio--which was also located in Turin--long after his early Ferrari creations had made him famous. The cozy cockpit of our Top Ten feature car, seen below, is completely original. The windshield, on the other hand, must have been an addition, as it does not appear in early pictures.

340 MEXICO

1952

Progenitor of Big Ferrari Power

The browning vignette to the right, catches the winning style of Bill Spear and his 340 Mexico. The team captured the SCCA championship in 1953. Seen below, Bill Spear flashing his victory smile, while Al Momo, the team mechanic, expresses a more subdued reaction to the frivolous mood of the winner's circle. Pictured further below, Phil Hill and friends, youthful and eager. Hill was Spear's co-driver in endurance events.

D eeply rooted in the Ferrari legend is the concept of invincibility. It is simply all too tempting to surrender to the notion that the road to success was always straight, and that victory was always a foregone conclusion. Nothing could be further from fact.

During 1950, the fledgling Ferrari firm experienced a crisis. The arena of sports car racing had seen the Prancing Horse perform with great bravura, but when it came to Formula One, Ferrari had fallen short of his ambition of forcing Alfa Romeo into submission.

As a result, the opinion was voiced that the supercharged 1500 cc unit—a development of Colombo's basic design—did not possess what was needed to achieve the total domination envisioned by Ferrari.

The champion of this position was Lampredi, who belabored the benefits of a big, normally-aspirated engine. Granted, the superchargers of the era were not only much too complex, but also much too thirsty.

Reports from America, where Chinetti had taken up position as the Ferrari agent, added fuel to Lampredi's contention. The American market was large and prosperous, and obviously one that could be effectively swayed by domestic racing successes.

But with the emergence of the big, formidable Cadillac and Chrysler power plants, Ferrari's prospects in America looked less than promising.

When it came down to a choice, Ferrari in the end sided with Lampredi, a decision that prompted Colombo to move back to Alfa Romeo. The stage was set for a new epoch, one dominated by Lampredi and his call for *big* power.

A urelio Lampredi came to Ferrari from a background in the aircraft industry. As an engineer, he initially worked for Piaggio, before changing to the legendary Reggiane-Caproni concern, where his talent was put to use designing engines, an assignment that taught him to value reliability.

Lampredi's new design paid homage to Colombo's brilliance through the fact that it built on the basic outline of his creation. But where Colombo had been flamboyant, Lampredi prescribed conservatism—strengthening, enlarging, simplifying.

The *big* Lampredi power plant came to be known as the *long* engine. This was due to the fact that Lampredi chose to space the cylinders further apart, thus allowing for expansion.

The most significant attribute of the new design, however,

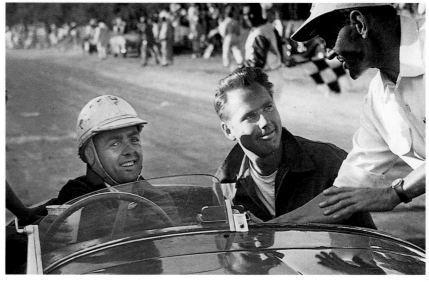

Lampredi increased power to an earth-shattering 280 hp, which produced the top speed of a monstrous 175 mph...

was the aspect that the separate cylinder heads had now been replaced by ones that were cast *en suite* with the block. This in effect ended the sealing problem that had plagued the Colombo power plant.

Another revision was seen in the incorporation of individual intake ports, a configuration that improved breathing.

The initial batch of engines sported a 3322 cc volume, and powered two vehicles entered in the 1950 Mille Miglia. Both were non-finishers.

As a source of power for the Grand Prix cars, the machine came frustratingly close to seeing Ferrari's ambitions fulfilled in 1951, but the team lost to Alfa in the last race of the season—a fact some saw as a vindication for Colombo, who had been responsible for the development of the Alfa racers.

The Lampredi engine fared somewhat better when shoehorned into sports racing cars. Increased to 4101 cc—producing the Tipo 340—the power plant propelled the Mille Miglia winner in 1951, thus prompting a Mille Miglia appellation.

The most potent of the 340 models, and the one that has attained an almost legendary status, was the Mexico, so called for its singular purpose, that of

competing in the 1952 Carrera Panamericana.

Power was increased to an earth-shattering 280 hp, through the deployment of three twin-throat 40 DCF Webers. The top speed—a monstrous 175 mph plus—was attained using a12/42 rear axle ratio and with the engine running at a lazy 6600 rpm. The compression was set at a reliable 8 to1.

Three coupes and one spyder were prepared, all bodied by Vignale, and all designed by the innovative Michelotti.

Underneath those aggressive shapes languished a tubular frame. Although the concept was new to Ferrari, it still utilized the traditional oval-section tubes, but the structure was raised to include the cowling and the front fenders. Otherwise, chassis and mechanical components comprised standard Ferrari fare, although with one important irregularity: the five-speed gear box was reintroduced. It had not been deployed since the 212, but was now deemed the perfect solution for those last long straightaways south of the Mexico-U.S. border.

Thus, conceived, built and prepared with the ultimate care and expectation of everyone involved, from Ferrari on down the line, the machines were shipped off to Mexico.

The long Lampredi engine was well set back in the Mexico's unique tubular chassis, and therefore required a long engine compartment and hood. This overview emphasizes the neat package which, underneath its twin Siluminum cylinder heads, hides a dozen steeply domed Borgo pistons, double overhead camshafts and a crankshaft running in seven Vandervell Thin-wall bearings. The twin Marelli magnetos protrude from the front, supplying a single set of spark plugs. Featured to the left, the screwed-in steel liners, showing their threaded upper ends.

All the King's Men. Enzo Ferrari and entourage listen to the phonetics of power during a test session at the factory in Maranello. The year is 1952. The men are, from left to right, Villoresi, Ugolini, Bassi and Ascari. The Commendatore himself wears his overcoat. Lampredi, creator of the machine, is on the right. Seen below, a birds-eye angle of Michelotti's creation, lean and long-hooded--six feet from windshield to grille.

Once the cars were released onto the wild and hazardous roads of Mexico, all the high hopes were soon savagely crushed...

There has over the years been some confusion among Ferrari historians as to whether the Mexico Spyder ever went to Mexico--or directly to Spear. The vignette on the right hand page, shows the Spyder on the loading dock of an Italian port. Visible behind it, is the hood of one of the coupes--proof positive that the Spyder indeed went the same way as the coupes. According to some sources, it was stripped for components during the race.

O nce the cars were released onto the wild and vicious roads of Mexico, however, those high hopes were soon savagely crushed. The scenario resembled a prelude of sorts to *Vanishing Point*, with one machine after the other disappearing from the score cards.

Already on the first leg, Ascari hit some loose rocks in a curve, rolled off the road and slammed into the embankment, crushing not only the front suspension but also one side of that delicate aluminum skin.

Then, on the leg from Mexico City via Leon to Durango, it was Villoresi's turn to bite the bullet, forced into retirement because of a broken rear axle.

Fortunately, after a stupendous effort on the last leg, Chinetti managed a third overall, giving the Man in Maranello a dose of consolation.

Also in running order at the end—but not because it managed to come through the ordeal in one piece, but because it never ran—was the spyder. The car had been reserved for American Bill Spear, who, for a reason that has now become obscured by the haze of history, failed to show up.

In a twist of irony, it fell to this lone spyder—certainly with the assistance from other big-banger Ferraris—to convert American

fans to the virtues of the new machines from Maranello.

In the hands of Spear, who had the car delivered to Florida, the potent machine—strikingly distinctive in its new blue and white livery—became one of the most successful competitors in Class C during that memorable SCCA season of 1953.

In February, the car, co-driven by Phil Hill, scored a second overall at McDill, Florida. In April, competing at Bergstrom, Texas, Spear captured first, while in Monterey, California, he had to settle for second. The season continued in much the same way, ending with Spear capturing the SCCA crown.

T he Mexico Spyder, despite its successful racing career, does not earn its Top Ten rating solely based on this criteria. As with the Rossellini/Bergman 212 Export, presented in the previous chapter, it is the work of Michelotti that gives it the push to the top.

This master of metal shaping reached his peak in the early fifties. He was the most dynamic, as well as the most productive of the Italian stylists of the era. Later, his work suffered from over-decoration.

But a stylist was only half a man without a panel-beater skillful enough to interpret his

The ferocious front end of the Mexico Spyder, provides proof of Michelotti's obsession with the fenders, which he elongated to the extreme. Although the theme was first seen on the cars built for the Carrera, it returned in subsequent Michelotti creations. Two such designs were built, one shown at the Geneva Salon in 1953, another at the Turin Salon that same year. The rear of the Spyder, left, was not as radical as the front.

Some of the major players are gone, but their spirit lives on in this embodiment of big Lampredi power and dazzling Michelotti style...

perceptions. In Alfredo Vignale, Giovanni Michelotti found such a partner. Both men had worked for Stabilimenti Farina, the Turin-based firm founded in 1905 by Giovanni Farina, the brother of Battista Farina—later to be known as Pinin Farina.

Michelotti, only sixteen, was first set to do odd jobs, but soon advanced to a responsibility of designing complete cars, finally maturing into the studio's star stylist. Vignale, beginning as a panel-beater, rose to department head, before setting up his own shop in 1946. A peculiar aspect of Vignale's working process was that he never used patterns, but a free-hand approach.

By 1949, it was Michelotti's turn to branch out, making his service available on a free-lance basis. This, to begin with, forced him to work out of the cramped quarters of his bedroom.

The Mexio design illustrates Michelotti's fascination with the front fenders, which now had become extended to the extreme. They were in fact so thin and pointed that there was no place for the headlights, thus their positioning on either side of the grille—a unique approach that created a ferocious look.

But Michelotti was not only an artist with an imaginative brush, he was endowed with a practical sense as well, and this side of

his talent caused him to take an interest in aerodynamics. One manifestation of this is found on the side panels of the Mexico cars, where Michelotti applied an elaborate combination of ailerons and ducts to funnel air to the rear brakes.

For years, the unique spyder, chassis number 0228 AT (A for America, T for Tubolare) was thought lost. Spear sold the machine to Alfred Momo. He in turn sold it to Philip Schwartz, who campaigned it for several years before passing it on to Ron Nardi—that was where the zig-zag trail ended.

Fortunately, the spyder has surfaced again, now owned by a collector in Mexico City. The car has recently gone through a complete restoration, executed under the watchful eye of Steve Tillack, of Tillack & Company, Harbor City, California.

Some of the major players are gone—Michelotti and Lampredi among them—but their spirit lives on in the body of their work. The product of these efforts was seldom expressed more quintessentially than in the breathtaking Mexico Spyder, where Ferrari's inspiration gave birth to a unique mix of big Lampredi power and dazzling Michelotti style.

The cockpit of the Mexico is, as it should be on a proper spyder, snug and functional, although perhaps not as comfortable as it appears--the spring perches protrude right below the seats, and can be felt through the cushions. The dash is clean, leaving few items to distract the vision, except the huge speedometer and tachometer gauges, with the latter located closest to the driver. The trunk holds little more than the spare wheel and the fuel tank, which has a 42 gallon capacity.

1954

pininfarina

Epitome of Enzo and Pinin Panache

Certainly, there was never a time when Ferrari did not have enough problems to keep his mind occupied. The early months of 1954 were therefore no different—only, perhaps, in regards to a fairly insignificant matter that passed across his desk a number of times before finally being resolved.

Early that year, Enzo Ferrari could look back on two extraordinary seasons of Grand Prix racing, culminating in his star driver, Alberto Ascari, rising to the top, capturing the World Championship crown in 1952, and again in 1953.

The 1954 season, however, began badly. Ferrari was faced with the loss of both Ascari and Villoresi to Lancia. Then, in the opening round, the Argentine Grand Prix, his best car placed no better than second. In the Syracuse Grand Prix, although Farina did manage a win, the bad luck continued, with two of his new cars being destroyed, Hawthorn's in a crash, and Gonzalez' in a fire.

There was, however, some consolation to be garnered from news bulletins transmitted from Buenos Aires and the 1000 km event for sports cars held there, where the Farina/Maglioli team drove Ferrari's latest creation, the super potent 375 Plus, to a welcome victory.

Between the erratic swells of pain and pleasure that kept washing in and out of Ferrari's consciousness flowed that endless stream of more or less important items requiring his attention. Among these, again, was that fairly insignificant matter that had already passed across his desk a number of times—the one that concerned an individual in California who had ordered a 375 MM sports racer for use on the road. It was the kind of deployment Ferrari looked upon with displeasure. He preferred to have every one of his siblings prowling race tracks in search of glory for the Prancing Horse.

Ferrari subsequently learned that this inquiry, channelled through West Coast race driver Jack McAfee, came from a woman, a fact that only served to increase his opposition to the transaction.

Ferrari's response, according to the story (which is founded on the recollections of one of the principals—an account that can no longer be corroborated), was to increase the price, thinking that this would stop the woman from further action.

The tactic did not produce the desired result, however, as the individual—the heir to a limitless fortune in oil—possessed more than ample means.

When Road & Track magazine wanted a car to feature on the cover of its November 1955 issue, editors turned to Jack McAfee, who supplied the yellow 375 MM that would thirty-five years later be our Top Ten choice. Glenn Embree was commissioned to do the photography. At the bottom of the page, Enzo Ferrari listens as one of his mechanics tunes the engine of a 375 MM. On this page, our Top Ten car seen in its unlikely Nevada hideout.

The 375 MM combines Ferrari's most formidable power plant to date with a Pinin Farina body that fades anything seen on the sports car horizon...

According to this account, Ferrari finally gave in, but made it clear that he did not want the car to be red. This color was just too distinctly associated with his competition cars.

So, Pinin Farina, in what could very likely have been the first such occurrence, picked a bright yellow for the exterior of the car, complementing this selection with a mossy shade of green for the seats and door panels, thus producing an effect that was both extraordinarily shocking as well as refreshingly harmonious. As for the yellow, it proved to be a choice that inspired a popular trend. On a different level, it turned out to create a controversy.

Out of this irregular order, however—controversial already from the beginning—emerged a survivor that stands out as one of the most superb among the early Ferraris. Still intact today, virtually untouched—hidden in a time capsule in Nevada—its claim to a Top Ten spot cannot be turned aside.

Seen as a model, the choice of the 375 MM materializes as equally clear-cut, mixing, as this machine does, Ferrari's most powerful engine to date with a Pinin Farina body that set a new standard for what a sports car should look like. The test of time, the most discriminating judge of good and bad, has only added to the stature of a design that today's admiring students of automotive styling considers Pinin Farina's first Ferrari masterpiece.

As far as the particular styling genealogy of the 375 MM Spyder is concerned, its roots can be traced to a berlinetta Pinin Farina built for privateer Kurt Zeller in 1953. This design featured *frenched* headlights, had prominently drawn-out front fenders, and a rectangular grille that slanted dramatically towards the lower edge, giving it a sharp, shark-like expression.

This style cropped up again on the 375 MM Berlinetta driven by Marzotto in the 1953 Carrera Panamericana. Only seven of these cars, all having similar body styles—but set apart by minor detail differences— were produced. A majority of the 375 MMs were shrouded in the spyder body. Altogether, exactly twenty-two topless cars of this particular body style were built by Pinin Farina.

Some Ferrari connoisseurs consider the berlinetta to be the most attractive. Others prefer the spyder body. In this writer's opinion, the spyder takes the top spot. The berlinetta design has a different fender line,

The color photographs above, focus the attention on the frontal treatment of Pinin Farina's first Ferrari masterpiece, the 375 MM. He initially employed this aggressive, shark-like theme on a berlinetta in 1953, but the originator of the style was Michelotti. In this spyder, the theme reached the level of the absolute. The rear, right, brings about a harmonious conclusion. To the left, our Top Ten feature, shown after completed restoration.

The spyder design projects an interplay between volumes and lines that is virtually impossible to improve upon...

one that eliminates the dip at the end of the cockpit, the feature that so evocatively interprets the waist and hip lines of a feline ready to pounce.

The spyder design features an interaction between volumes and lines that seems virtually impossible to improve. Giving the eyes further provocation are elements such as the hood blister, with its representation of awesome, bulging, muscular might duplicated on the trunk lid in a gesture to symmetry. Lured to the tail end, the eyes catch the huge filler cap that forms, as it were, a punctuation mark to the entire design.

In a final burst of brilliance, as if anything—anything at all— was lacking, Pinin Farina elects to leave a trail of exposed rivets sprinkled across the hood, all in an articulate endorsement of function as the true inspiration for all good design.

Beneath the advanced shell of aluminum hid a frame and suspension setup that was, in contrast, conventional—in fact aging—as the chassis had seen little development since the days of the 166 Barchetta.

The frame, manufactured from welded tubular steel, was still suspended via transverse leaf springs up front and semi-elliptical springs at the rear.

Furthermore, it still employed Houdaille shock absorbers in all four corners. The brakes were of course still of the dependable, but somewhat inadequate, drum variety.

As far as its direct lineage, the chassis came from the 342 America, incorporating a four-speed all-synchromesh gearbox, heavy-duty differential, and a 2600 mm wheelbase.

It was all pretty basic, and although functional, not that well-equipped to handle all the awesome power produced by Lampredi's latest barrage of development, which brings us to the engine. As always, in the case of Ferrari, the power plant occupied a central role in the engineering philosophy.

The 375-configuration came as a result of new bore and stroke dimensions, now fixed at 84 mm by 68 mm. The new displacement figure was 4522 cc. With breathing handled by the triumvirate of four-throat 40 IFC/4 downdraft Webers, the machine produced 340 hp at 7000 rpm.

The acceleration numbers were also improved. The zero-to-sixty figure no longer rested in the ten-second range, as had been the case with the 166, nor was it in the seven-second zone, as with the 212, but in the five-second bracket.

The 375, in its ultimate form--with the engine capacity of 4954 cc, and the *Plus* addendum--brought Le Mans glory to Ferrari in 1954 for the first time since Chinetti's 1949 win. The clipping and the faded photograph, add the aura of nostalgia to our presentation, as Froilan Gonzalez and his mount shoot past the grandstands in a spray of water during the rain-soaked ordeal. Gonzalez set a new lap record with an average speed of 117 mph.

The black and white illustrations to the left are Ferrari publicity photographs number 108 and 109, dated March 27, 1954--seven days after completion of chassis 0398. The color pictures, above, add straight-on front and side views to the three-quarter angles provided by the Ferrari factory shots. The side view shows the sensual flow of the fender line, which begins at the nose, sweeps back and dips to a waist, before descending towards the tail--pure animal inspiration.

The irreverent owner used to drive the gate guards of the exclusive community crazy by passing below the still-lowered boom...

The view of the rear, below, shows the thoughtful Pinin Farina touch, which, with its bulge on the trunk lid, repeats the shape of the blister on the hood. It neatly embraces the huge filler cap, which opens up to a tank that swallows upwards of 42 gallons. Further below, a birds-eye view of the cockpit. The minimal door invites the driver to a compartment that, thanks to the tonneau cover, creates an all-enveloping feeling.

With the machine running at top speed, the speedometer needle would settle not very far from the 180 mph mark. No wonder Ferrari had doubts when he visualized a woman using his high-strung racing thoroughbred to go shopping, although it may have been to Bonwit Teller rather than to the local grocery store.

Our Top Ten selection is a typical example of the 375 MM spyders as delivered to private customers, with the first of the batch sold to American Jim Kimberly, who used it to win his SCCA crown.

Completed in September of 1953, this unit was followed by another in October. By the following January, a similar car had been built for Spear, in which he won at the March Air Force Base. In May, the next 375 MM was ready for delivery to John Edgar. In the hands of McAfee, this machine captured first place in the Golden Gate sports car event.

The last 375 MM Spyder is our feature car, chassis 0460 AM, which had been completed for shipment to the West Coast by September of 1954.

By this time, Ferrari had made his own creation obsolete by issuing the 375 Plus, which, with its de Dion rear axle and its

gearbox placed in the rear for improved weight distribution, was a much-enhanced racing tool—in spite of the fact that another displacement increase, to 4954 cc, resulted in only four more horses.

The Plus was the car in which Gonzalez managed to beat the Jaguars at Le Mans in 1954, thus returning Ferrari to the winner's circle for the first time since Chinetti's 1949 win.

What is known about the subsequent adventures of number 0460? Not very much. It seems to have lived a quiet life, used, as was the plan, for occasional transportation by the same woman who wanted it so bad she was willing to pay a premium to own it.

In this capacity, the car was first stationed in Beverly Hills. At one point, the machine was very nearly destroyed when the garage where it was usually housed burned to the ground. Luckily, owner and car were at the time away on a weekend trip. Only its tonneau cover was destroyed.

Later, 0460 was domiciled in posh Pebble Beach, where its irreverent owner used to drive the gate guards of the exclusive community crazy by passing beneath the still-lowered boom, naturally without stopping—all

Above, the engine of one of the three 375 MMs campaigned by Ferrari during 1953. In this configuration the machine sported a displacement of 4494 cc. When the customer version arrived in the fall of the same year, the displacement had been expanded slightly, to 4522 cc. To the left, the engine compartment of our Top Ten car. Note the black crackle-paint cylinder heads--this could mark the first use of a finish that later became the norm.

Its location remains a secret, and prospective buyers should be aware that the car is not for sale, never was...

that was required could be done in a fast nod that dipped one's head down below that minimal wind screen.

With the increasing age of the proprietor, chassis 0460 was seldom exercised and sat idle in its garage for long periods of time, gathering dust.

At the time of the owner's death, her son took over title to the car and it was at this point, in the early seventies, that a decision was made to administer a complete restoration.

Everett Adams, a craftsman formerly employed by Harrah's Auto Collection, had recently established his own restoration business in Reno, and, based on this track record, was chosen for the delicate job.

It presented no problem to verify the true specifications of the car, since nothing had ever been altered—a fact the new owner could corroborate, since he had not only accompanied his mother on many excursions in the car, but had also been present when the machine was unloaded from a ship in the San Pedro harbor.

Adams proceeded with great prudence, taking special care to preserve the original condition and configuration of every part of the car. In fact, the only object that required remaking was the special aluminum tonneau cover

that had been destroyed in the Beverly Hills fire.

Upon its completion in 1973, the car was invited to take part in the prestigious Concours de Elegance in Pebble Beach. Nineteen years had passed since the question of its disposition had been decided by Enzo, and since Pinin made his choice of color. It was time for controversy once again.

The Concours judges, in a decision that left a blemish on a respected event, judged the colors a minus, despite the fact that fidelity could be proven beyond a doubt.

The owner, robbed of a fair judging, returned to Nevada, determined never to display the rare survivor again. For close to seventeen years, it remained locked up in a location known to just two individuals—until freed for this Top Ten photograpy session. It has now been returned to its solitary confinement.

Its location is again a secret, and prospective suitors should know that the car is not for sale, never was, not when it stood abandoned, nor at a time when it was rejected by the judges, nor today, when its worth is truly recognized—not only in terms of money—but in terms of a status as one of the all-time most desirable Ferraris.

375 PLUS SPECIALE

1955

King of Brute Power and Posh Beauty

Our Top Ten feature car was built for King Leopold of Belgium, seen here in 1935, after the funeral of his wife, the Swedish Princess Astrid. At his side are Princess Josephine Charlotte, and Prince Baudouin who, at the age of eighteen, ascended to the throne vacated by his father's 1951 abdication. Leopold was an avid car enthusiast, and is said to have owned a Bugatti in the thirties. In the fifties, he became one of Ferrari's early customers.

In the August 1969 issue of *Car and Driver* magazine, an ad offered a 1955 Ferrari for sale. The model was described as a Superamerica.

The text went on to describe the vehicle as a convertible, in like-new condition, powered by a 2.5-liter engine, and having been previously owned by King Leopold of Belgium.

A photograph provided a representation of the automobile. Long-hooded and lean, it was parked nonchalantly beside the curb of a city street.

The seller indeed listed an address in Brussels, the capital of Belgium, as the source for additional information. Judging from this fact, the assertion of its royal connection seemed plausible. Except, to the eyes of a long-time Ferrari enthusiast in Chicago who happened to spot the ad, the car did not look like any Superamerica he had ever seen. Nor, as far as this expert could recall, had King Leopold ever owned a Superamerica.

The enthusiast, Ed Andrews, was, however, well aware of a one-off Pinin Farina cabriolet built for the king.

Andrews had in fact chased the automobile for years, but had always lost the trail before being able to act on the lead. This time, however—although not in the position to buy it—he was determined to follow up, and paid a visit to fellow enthusiast, Wayne Golomb.

The two had often discussed the car and Golomb, fresh out of law school, had already been making plans for an extended vacation—a trip that would take him to Europe in search of an exotic Ferrari.

He immediately packed his bags, which included a special tool-and-parts kit assembled by Andrews, and took the next flight to Brussels—but without contacting the seller.

King Leopold III, who had assumed the duties as ruler of Belgium in 1934 when his father, Albert I, met his death in a climbing accident, lived a life full of controversy.

In the early summer of 1940, with the Nazis on the prowl, Hitler's blitzkrieg attack forced Belgium's government to flee. King Leopold, however, against the suggestion of his cabinet, chose to stay. As commander of the army, he led the resistance against the invasion force. Then, unexpectedly—although it was indeed a hopeless battle—the king decided to capitulate after only eighteen days, a highly controversial decision, and one many condemned as akin to enemy collaboration.

King Leopold's Ferrari ended up in the U.S. as a result of an advertisement placed in the August 1969 issue of Car and Driver magazine, a facsimile of which is shown to the right. The photograph below, shows the car as it stands today. Considered the most beautiful luxury road Ferrari ever produced, its owner for more than two decades, Wayne Golomb, spent the better part of a decade and a half on bringing it back to life.

FERRARI

FOR SALE—FERRARI SUPER-AMERICA like new. Convertible, 1955 PI 2.5 lts. engine. Previously owned by H. M. King Leopold Exclusive model. For all ...
... 402

The king ran out of road, grazed a tree, and plunged into the icy waters of the lake, accidentally killing the young queen...

Leopold spent the rest of the war in German imprisonment. With Allied forces crushing the final Nazi resistance in 1945, he became a free man. Because of the continuing controversy at home, however, Leopold was not able to return until 1950, after a referendum indicated a majority support.

The wounds had not healed, however. Strikes and rioting soon broke out, threatening to tear the country apart. King Leopold was left with no other option than to abdicate. His son, Baudouin, barely eighteen, became the new ruler.

This controversy, however, was not the first to scandalize Leopold's reign. In 1926, at a time when he was still a prince, he had married the beautiful Astrid, a Swedish princess, who bore him three children.

With her charm and beauty, Astrid captured the hearts of her new subjects, and was soon embraced with affection as a national treasure.

Tragedy struck in 1935, when the king—whose affection for sporty cars and spirited driving was well-known—en route from Switzerland, ran out of road, grazed a tree, and plunged into a lake, accidentally killing the queen. National sentiment held the monarch responsible, and never quite forgave him.

Years later, as a prisoner of war, King Leopold once again generated controversy when he married Liliane Baels. Not only a commoner, she was also three months pregnant at the time.

By the mid-fifties, the former ruler and his new wife, who had now acquired a name and a title worthy of royalty—Princess Liliane de Rethy—had settled into their new life. It was a life that lacked nothing, including the indulgence in fast and fabulous automobiles.

Leopold purchased his first Ferrari in 1952, a 342 America, which was one of the earliest Pinin Farina bodies executed on a Ferrari chassis, and had a rather oversized grille.

The year of 1955 saw the couple take delivery of a pair of brand new Ferraris. The one for the princess was a Vignale-built 250 GT; the one for the king, a Pinin Farina-bodied 375 Plus Speciale—the latter, the particular object of Andrew's and Golomb's interest.

This one-of-a-kind automobile, its chassis stamped with an even number—0488 AM—and commonly referred to as the *King Leopold Ferrari,* reached a chassis-stage of completion at the Maranello factory during the last days of 1954.

An intriguing record exists

The browning photograph to the left captures King Leopold and his beautiful Ferrari 375 Speciale at an unspecified race track, probably in Belgium. It can be conjectured that the king put in a lap or two in a graceful gesture to the spectators. A close scrutiny reveals that the car sports three-winged hubs. These were the type used on the Formula racers, but were now drilled and secured by wires--presumably at the request of the king.

The engine was derived directly from a configuration specially developed for use during the 1951 Formula One season...

of this occasion, with the naked chassis being photographed just as the contraption sets out on its maiden voyage. Grand Prix seats were temporarily installed for driver and passenger, and the entire scene looks rather like the staging of a daredevil act, especially so when one realizes that the car was not a docile, run-of-the-mill road machine—as if any Ferrari can be referred to as docile and run-of-the-mill—but one powered by an all-out racing engine.

This formidable machine, the prodigy of the thoroughbred Lampredi lineage—and derived directly from a configuration developed in particular for use during the 1951 Formula One season—was not the same as the power plant deployed in other 375 MMs. That is, not the version used by Scuderia Ferrari sports racing cars in 1953, and not the engine found in customer 375 MMs sold from late 1953 to late 1954. It was actually the same unit as the one powering the factory team cars in 1954, which was a model identified as 375 MM Plus—the same machine that played a major role in the battle that brought Ferrari that year's World Championship title for manufacturers.

The Plus engine featured the same 84 mm bore as the normal 375 unit, but sported a stroke

that had been lengthened from 68 mm to 74.5 mm, resulting in a displacement increase that went from 4522 cc to 4954 cc. The compression ratio was 9 to 1, and power output about 340 hp at 7000 rpm. Air was provided by three huge Webers, designated 46DCF3.

In his book, *Ferrari*, Hans Tanner lists a set of performance figures that, if correct, illustrate the phenomenal performance of the 375 Plus. Temporarily fitted with huge eighteen-inch wheels, and the most long-legged of its rear axle ratios, the machine managed zero to sixty in four seconds, and a top speed in fourth gear of an awesome 210 mph—figures that make today's sports cars pale.

T he chassis of the Leopold Ferrari was different in many other ways as well. It featured its steering wheel located on the left side. Only one other unit is known to have been delivered this way. It was also the first road car to feature coil springs in its front suspension.

The photograph of the naked chassis also provides clues indicating that certain changes were made once the unit had reached Pinin Farina. One such alteration originated with the need for a lower hood line, and was accomplished by fitting

The engine powering the King Leopold Ferrari, was of the same configuration as the ones installed in the four 375 Plus sports racing cars that constituted the Ferrari factory team in 1954--the 4954 cc version. With a trio of double-throat 42DCF Weber carburetors, and a 9 to 1 compression ratio, output was a stunning 344 hp --plus. Reproduced on the previous page, a facsimile of the king's personal registration document, dated July 28, 1955.

The Leopold Ferrari speaks most eloquently, not only of the men responsible for its creation, but also of the man to whose fine taste it was tailored...

a one-inch shorter, single-piece air-cleaner unit.

Other changes indicate that King Leopold might have tested the car before taking delivery, and that he found certain details not to his liking.

One of the alterations that might have resulted from such a test was the relocation of the rear-view mirror, which originally occupied a position on top of the dash and later was moved to a position at the top of the windshield frame. This alteration was obviously necessitated by the fact that the bulk of the soft top, when folded, obscured the view completely.

A more radical change, also thought to have been caused by the king's trying out his brand new Ferrari, had to do with the obvious lack of leg room in the driver's compartment. During the restoration, it was discovered that the location of all the pedals had been moved forward as much as four inches.

Further alterations, probably also prompted by Leopold's test drive, concerned the brakes, where standard Ferrari drums were exchanged in favor of Al-Fin drums up front. This type was identical to the ones fitted on the Grand Prix racing cars during the 1955 season.

A four-speed, all-synchromesh transmission, and a six-plate clutch, featuring a larger surface area to enable it to handle the substantial increase in torque, finished the picture of a car that, engine and chassiswise, was a pure race car.

In summary, considering the outstanding specifications of the King Leopold Ferrari, one must say that the car speaks most eloquently, not only of the men responsible for its creation, but also of the man to whose taste it was tailored.

It certainly required a special stature to generate the degree of cooperation displayed by the Commendatore in this case. And it certainly also required an individual well versed in the language of power and speed. The king qualified in both of these categories.

It is known that Leopold played the role of middle-man during Ferrari's relationship with Englebert, the Belgian tire manufacturer, and that Enzo's attentiveness may have been a response to this. Be that as it may, King Leopold still had to shell out a sum equivalent to sixteen thousand dollars.

The attributes that elevate the King Leopold Ferrari to its Top Ten position, do not concern the engineering aspect alone. This factor, as can be seen from

Carrozzeria Pininfarina photographic archive number 684, seen to the left, shows a straight-on view of the Leopold Ferrari. Today, the survivor still appears the same, except for two non-authentic items: the headlight covers. These were originally made of glass, and were unique to the car. While Golomb has one of the original covers, he has not yet managed to find a firm able to duplicate it, and the ones presently on the car are made from Plexiglas.

While there were many designs leading to this stage, it was really first with the Leopold Ferrari that the Ferrari style finally unfolded into full bloom...

King Leopold apparently liked a car to be well equipped--evidenced by the photographs on this spread. In addition to the standard gauges, the dash also includes a chronometer (mounted in the center), and an altimeter (set in the glove box). The leather interior was originally beige, and while a show judge might fault Golomb for the choice of green, it adds pizzazz, and was, as a matter of fact, quite often specified by Pinin Farina.

the foregoing, indeed reflects state-of-the-art racing technology, but is matched in significance by the stature of the remarkable Pinin Farina styling.

Battista Farina was born in Turin in 1893, the tenth of eleven children. At the age of eleven, he began working in his brother Giovanni's workshop, the firm that became known as Stabilimenti Farina.

In 1930, Battista, who would become world famous by his nickname, Pinin, branched out on his own. The younger Farina rapidly gained a reputation for his outstanding coachwork that graced all the classic Italian marques—Alfa Romeo, Isotta-Fraschini and Lancia.

Pinin Farina's efforts during the first decade as his own master brought him in contention with the best in the business. But it was not until after the end of World War II that he rose to a position of industry leadership.

It was all accomplished in one breathtaking stroke that set the tone for automotive styling in the postwar era—the sweeping 1947 Cisitalia—perhaps his most enduring masterpiece.

The collaboration between Farina and Ferrari began rather late. The first example was a 1952 212 Inter. The early efforts lacked distinction, and it would

take a couple of years before Pinin had developed the unique look that could be called the Ferrari style.

While there were a number of designs leading up to this period, it was with the Leopold Ferrari that the Ferrari style finally unfolded into full bloom. Already present was the low, broad hood, the wide, elliptical grille, the arching, covered headlights—from here on it was a matter of refining the theme, a phase that continued into the mid-sixties.

At that time, a new approach in chassis layout necessitated a redefinition of the Ferrari style. The grille contracted gradually, the greenhouse moved towards the middle. The classic Ferrari style was lost.

But, back to the Leopold Ferrari. During the flight to Brussels, Golomb worried about not having been in contact with the seller before he left. What if the car had been sold?

The worrying proved to have been unnecessary.

The seller turned out to be a dealer, and Golomb first saw the Ferrari squeezed in among other exotics. Apparently it had been handed down through several owners after leaving the king's service. At one point, the vehicle had spent two years

Pininfarina, in an interview before his death in 1966, called the King Leopold Ferrari: The One That Never Ages...

abandoned on the street. And it all certainly showed.

A verification of documents and plates revealed an even chassis number—normally given only to race cars. The chassis type number was 102—normally denoting the Mille Miglia. The engine carried number 113— a designation given only to the 375 Plus motor.

All this was confusing at the time. In time, however, all the contradictions would be cleared up. But, for now, it was enough to know that the car was indeed the King's Ferrari. Golomb had reached the end of the road. The survivor he and Andrews had been looking for had finally been located. Question was, should he buy or not buy?

Golomb had hoped—with help from the tool kit—to use the Ferrari for a tour of Europe. A lack of power, hostile backfiring, and a slipping clutch put the idea out of his mind.

Golomb instead bought a Volkswagen and set course due south. But the Ferrari was not easily forgotten. Twice he turned north. Twice he turned south.

Two weeks passed. Golomb paid a visit to see the Ferrari factory, among other attractions. But the Leopold Ferrari would not leave his mind. Turning north, he decided on one last look—if it was still there?

That last look, however, was to be a lasting one. This time Golomb bought the car, paying $12,000 in cash.

A few months later, Golomb and Andrews watched the car being unloaded from a freighter in Calumet Harbor.

Now remained only the final phase—the restoration—a task that would occupy a period of almost fifteen years.

The epic effort brought back to life the King Leopold Ferrari in all its royal glory, and as such was an accomplishment worthy of the most beautiful road Ferrari ever conceived.

King Leopold died in 1983, at the age of 81. On a number of occasions Golomb, corresponding with the aid of an intermediary, communicated with the King, who expressed his satisfaction over the fact that the car was again owned by a true enthusiast.

Pininfarina, in an interview before his death in 1966, called the Leopold Ferrari: *The One That Never Ages.*

More than thirty-five years have gone by since the creation of this fast and beautiful Ferrari built for a king. With its blend of the ultimate of two disciplines— racing technology and styling artistry—it is still the King of Posh Beauty and Brute Power.

If public recognition is a tribute to excellence, then Golomb and his Leopold Ferrari have certainly received their reward--honors shared with his mother and father, who were involved from the start. In the photo above, snapped after the 1985 Meadowbrook Concours de Elegance, Michigan, the Golombs celebrate capturing the award for Best Sports Car of Show--the result of formidable Ferrari power, sublime Pinin Farina artistry, and never-fading Golomb devotion.

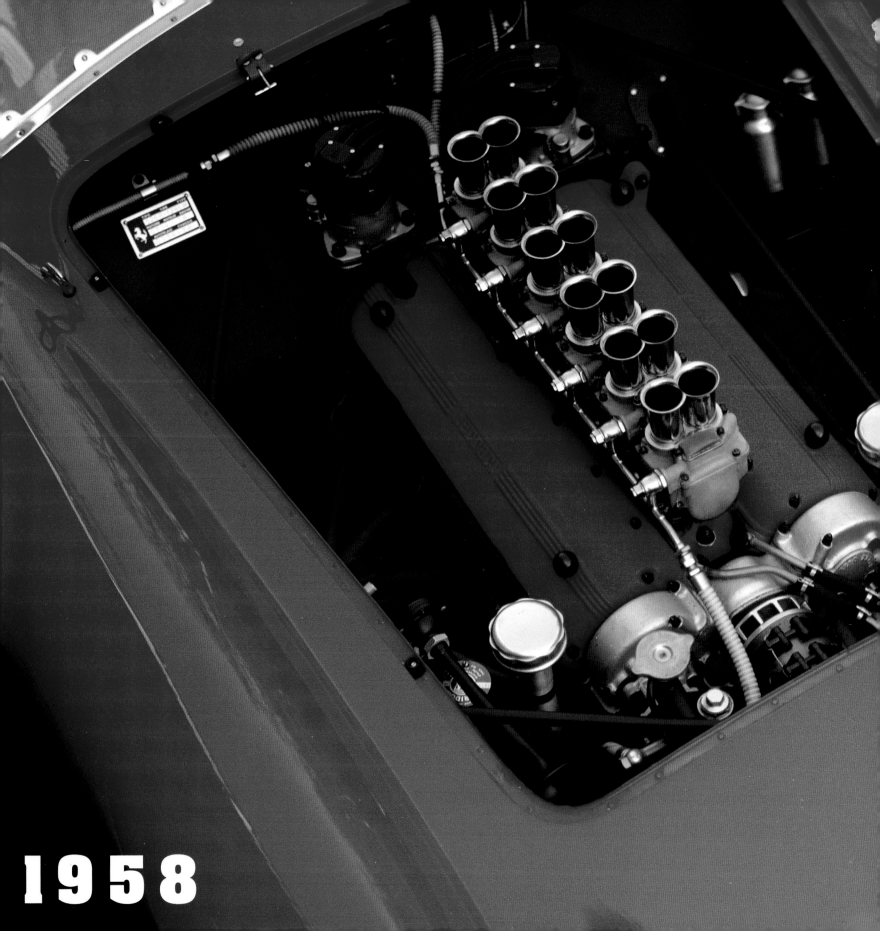

1958

250 TESTA ROSSA

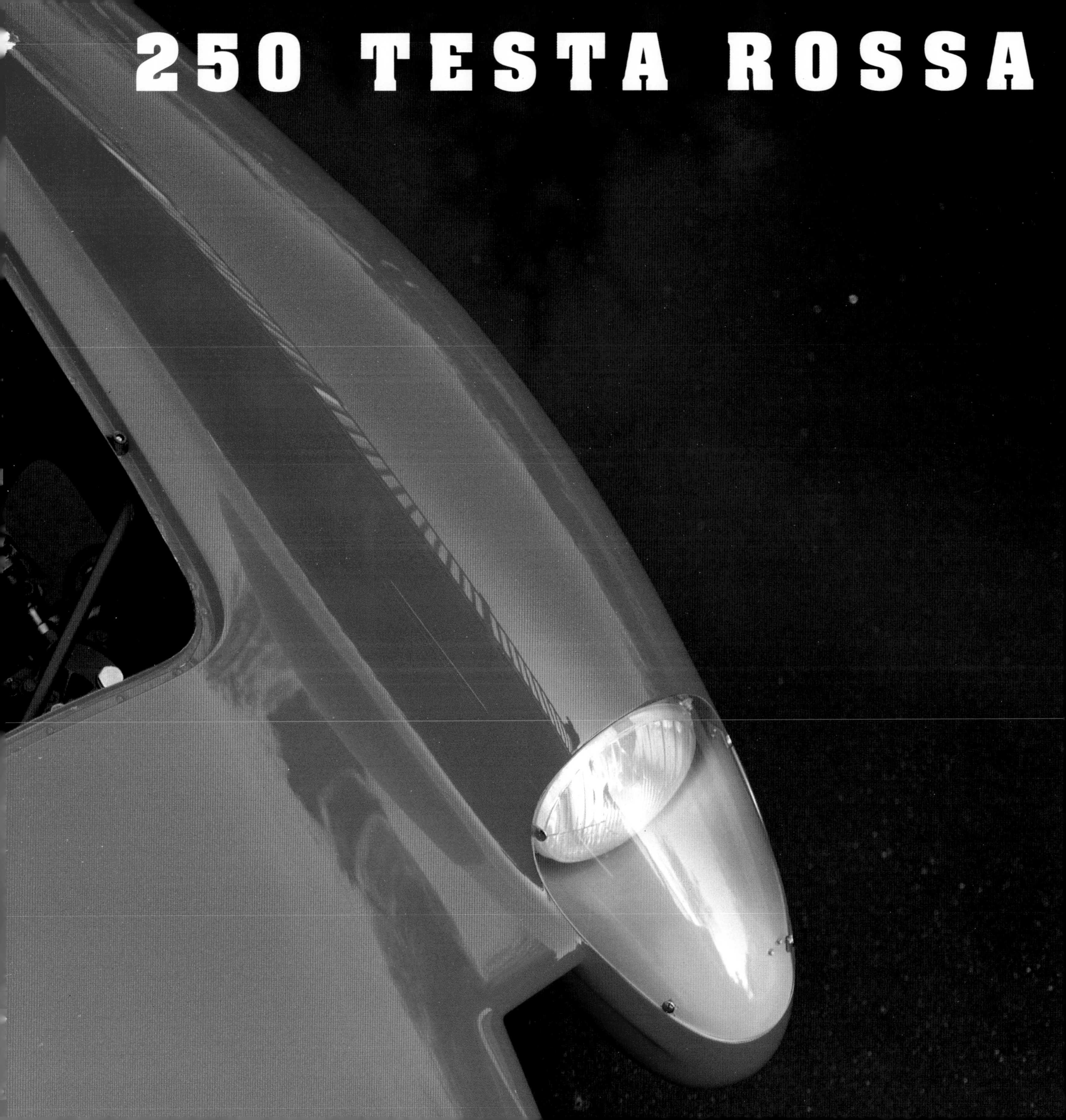

Pontoon Fendered Star Performer

A cockpit does not get much better than the Testa Rossa's. The wooden steering wheel, the black gauges, the gated shift lever--it's all there. Opposite page, a view of the complete machine in all its awesome glory--wide and flat like a monster. To the right, a rare find in a news magazine published late in 1958; the clipping--alive with excitement--shows the first customer Testa Rossa boarding its Sabena flight to New York.

One of the secrets behind the success of Enzo Ferrari was his intimate knowledge of the machinery that makes the public relations carousel move. His media extravaganzas were always carefully orchestrated, and therefore enthusiastically covered by journalists.

The Ferrari press conference of November 22, 1957, held in Modena was, seen in retrospect, of particular interest.

For his centerpiece, Ferrari had chosen the new 250 TR, its TR designation referring to the Italian equivalent of *Red Head,* or *Testa Rossa,* a name in turn derived from the red crackle paint used to finish the cylinder heads of the Ferrari racing engines.

What the gathering of motor journalists witnessed was not a flash out of the blue. The 250 Testa Rossa had been tested extensively, both with regards to its body, built by Scaglietti, as well as its engine, a 3000 cc derivative of the fundamental Colombo design. With the two prototypes having already put in a number of appearances, perhaps the most visible being third and fourth place finishes in Caracas, the machine was a familiar quantity.

What constituted news at this point, however, was the fact that the occasion marked the introduction of a customer version of the 250 Testa Rossa. The car on display, chassis 0710, was in fact the first such unit, bought by Ferrari's U.S. West Coast distributor, John von Neumann, who immediately after the press showing had his silver beauty air-freighted to New York for further shipment to Florida by truck, and on to Nassau by boat.

After all that trouble, the machine—in the hands of Richie Ginther—did not make it to the finish line of the Nassau Speed Week main event.

The appearance in Nassau was the first outing of a privately-owned and entered Testa Rossa. Although it was not a successful one, it marked the beginning of an era that would bring lasting fame to the Testa Rossa appellation.

Most of the superstar glory, however, would come from the subsequent development of the Testa Rossa factory team cars, which, in the course of the 1958 to 1961 World Sports Car Championship seasons, would rack up a record of no less than ten victories out of twenty such races contested, win three times at Le Mans, and take the title in 1958, 1960 and 1961.

Ferrari's customers did not do badly either, capturing a fourth

74

It was discovered that one car had never as much as rolled on a race track, but had lived a life in complete celibacy...

in Argentina, and a fifth and a sixth at Le Mans—both in 1958. The privateer Testa Rossas saw their most extensive use in the United States, however, with class victories at Daytona and Riverside—both in 1959.

Of the thirty-four 250 Testa Rossas built, nineteen were of the customer configuration. As ambassadors of the Prancing Horse, these cars could hardly have been distributed more strategically had the allocation been done by Enzo himself; seven were bought by privateers in the United States; Venezuela, Italy and Belgium became home to two per nation; customers in Austria, Brazil, Cuba, Finland, Guatemala and Switzerland purchased one each.

The task of weeding out a Top Ten finalist from the nineteen proved to be something of a problem. In searching for a car with the most outstanding racing history, it was realized that, as a rule, the machines having seen service on the track had been drastically altered—which meant the appearance of a minus in the originality column.

Consider the following: nine examples had been robbed of their original power plants (one over-zealous owner had gone so far as to install an American V-8), three had been rebodied, and one had fallen victim to a fire—all this in addition to the numerous repairs to frames, suspensions and bodies that had become necessary due to various accidents.

The ideal combination of racing eminence and originality proved, as one would expect, impossible to find. The choice, it seemed, would have to be the example displaying the least scars, and this was indeed the approach until it was discovered that one car had never been seen on the race tracks but had in fact lived for two decades in complete celibacy, hidden away from the eyes of the world in a Stamford, Connecticut garage. This survivor then, if possible to locate, would be first choice for the Top Ten position.

The Testa Rossa provided a vehicle for the revival of the Colombo engine. The loyal servant, having already seen a decade of service, had been enlarged to 2953 cc, with its new bore and stroke dimensions fixed at 73 mm by 58.8 mm. Breathing through no less than six twin-choke Webers, its power had increased to 300 hp at 7200 rpm. The top speed varied depending on gearing. In its most long-legged configuration, the TR managed a brisk 170 mph. The acceleration could be

Pictured on the previous page, the 250 Testa Rossa, chassis 0754. Sold to Guatemalan Jaroslav Juhan, and driven by him and Francois Picard, the car came to grief after six hours of racing in the 1958 Le Mans. Left, Pedro Rodrigues at Riverside in 1959. He did not bring home his mount, chassis 0718, due to ignition problems. Our Top Ten feature, below, chassis 0734, looks immaculate while admiring its own reflection--it never raced.

1958 FERRARI 250 TESTA ROSSA

The Testa Rossa was not the result of a revolutionary design philosophy. It all followed the Ferrari tradition, which favored reliability over notability...

called blistering—zero-to-one hundred was expedited in less than sixteen seconds.

Thus updated, the Colombo machine was mated to a frame essentially similar to a design featured in the earlier 500 TRC, the four-cylinder car that had introduced the use of the Testa Rossa name in 1956.

This frame, although not as radical and complicated as the designs used in the Mercedes Gullwing and the little Maserati Birdcage, was of the multi-tube configuration as well.

The remainder of the chassis included conventional Ferrari fare, such as independent front suspension, using coil springs; and live rear axle, featuring semi-elliptical springs.

The brakes were still of the drum variety, and the gear-box, an all-synchromesh four-speed, was still up front.

All this, certainly, did not add up to a revolutionary design. It was all in the Ferrari tradition, which favored reliability over notability—a trait that served the machines from Maranello well in endurance racing.

When it came to the styling, however, conventionalism had been left by the roadside. As already mentioned, the Testa Rossa bodies were built by a small Modena firm by the name of Carrozzeria Scaglietti. This was not out of the ordinary, since the firm had been building racing bodies for Ferrari for some time, beginning in 1953 with the 750 Monza, which had been a collaborative effort with Enzo's son Dino.

The unique aspect, however, was that the Testa Rossa was styled not by Pinin Farina but by Sergio Scaglietti.

Scaglietti, whose business grew out of a body repair shop he founded in 1951, was not an artist with pen and paper in the conventional fashion found in the established styling studios of the day. In fact, those tools and supplies did not even exist in Scaglietti's arsenal, which was instead stocked with hammers and blow torches.

Sergio Scaglietti's method of creation consisted of building a cage, or *gabbia* in Italian, from flexible metal rods around the chassis, thus projecting a full-size, three-dimensional image of the car he visualized before his inner eyes.

Once Scaglietti was satisfied with the shape it was a matter of manufacturing the aluminum panels to fit the pattern, a task performed in the old-fashioned way—by hand and hammer on a tree stump or a sandbag.

For the Testa Rossa design, Scaglietti derived his inspiration

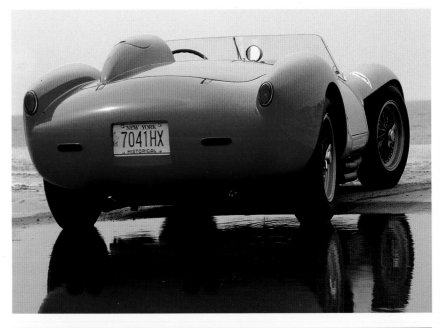

Scaglietti opened a space between the front fenders and the center portion of the body, thus allowing air to penetrate directly to the brake drums...

The color photographs on this spread capture the Scaglietti lines--shapes that spelled speed. Below, the birds-eye view of the Testa Rossa's front end reveals the elongated tear-drop theme that permeated virtually every part of the body, exemplified by the fenders and the hood blister and, in the photograph to the right, also the head fairing--doing double duty as cover for a filler cap that opened up to a fuel tank swallowing 37 gallons.

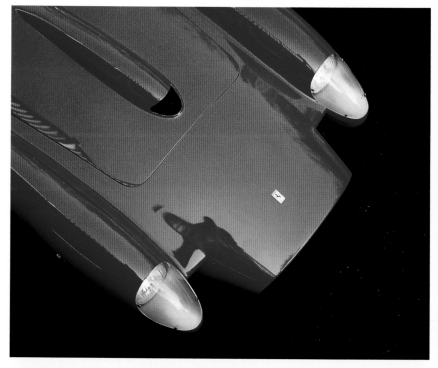

from the predecessor 500 TRC, which was penned and panelled by Carrozzeria Touring. This design featured an open front wheel well that swept rearward in a smooth curve. Pinin Farina had used a similar motif on a special body built for American *Gentleman Jim* Kimberly. In this case, the openings extended back even further and were repeated at the rear.

Scaglietti interpreted these designs in his own way, and in the process came up with a styling theme that captured the imagination of a generation of sports car enthusiasts—and to this day continues to draw raving comments.

But Scaglietti's inspiration did not stem only from the Touring and Pinin Farina efforts, but, perhaps to a larger extent, from airflow considerations. It was a matter of grave importance to funnel as much air as possible to brakes and radiator.

This concern also guided his design of the front end, where he placed a huge opening low to the ground, extending it to a snout-like appendage—all, as it was thought, allowing the maximum exposure to the flow of the airstream.

In addition, Scaglietti also opened up the space between the fenders and the main section of the body, thus forcing air

to penetrate directly to the front brake drums. This imparted a visual effect to the fenders which resembled pontoons. Thus was coined a phrase that would stick: *Pontoon Fender Ferrari.*

Scaglietti's design, although stunning from a visual viewpoint, proved less than satisfactory from an aerodynamic viewpoint, and factory Testa Rossas soon reverted to a more conventional body design.

One viewer, whose opinion counts—industrial design genius Raymond Loewy—once told Scaglietti, after having seen the Testa Rossas in action at Le Mans, that he felt sure it was a design that would stand up to the test of time.

And that it has—to such a degree that a copy of the master piece today is valued in the millions of dollars.

The mysterious, cloistered Top Ten Testa Rossa, the one that had never set wheels on a race track, was—in the course of the research for this book— first discovered through a repair bill from Chinetti Motors, the classic Ferrari dealership located in Stamford, Connecticut.

This document, dated June 26, 1975, and detailing a repair and restoration costing close to fourteen thousand dollars, pin- pointed the name of the man

Sergio Scaglietti was the humble craftsman responsible for the daring shapes that made the Testa Rossa such a stunner--then and now. Above, Scaglietti poses for the camera, with the always-present Nazionale cigarette firmly clipped between thumb and forefinger. The photograph was taken in the late sixties, at a time when his firm built the Daytona. Pictured on the previous page, bottom, a scene from Scaglietti's shop in the late fifties, during the era when he was Ferrari's coachbuilder of choice for the race cars, a time when the bodies were still built in the old traditional way--by hand and hammer.

The most original Testa Rossa in existence—the Virgin—still lives a life in seclusion...

The black and white illustration at the bottom of this page, shows Richie Ginther plugging his ears while he lets the engine warm up at 6500 rpm. Notice that the red-line on Ginther's tachometer is set at 8500 rpm, while the same instrument on our Top Ten feature car, below, is set at 7000. At the top of the opposite page, Ginther is negotiating turn six on the Laguna Seca track in 1958. He managed to capture a fine third.

who owned the Testa Rossa at the time: F. H. Gibbs. Both serial and engine numbers were also listed: 0734 and 0734—a perfect match, as it should be.

Recorded as well was Gibbs' address in New York. A phone call provided a lead to a retired employee of Gibbs' firm, who in turn—at the opposite end of a receiver—graciously shed some light on the existence of the mysterious Gibbs.

Frederick H. Gibbs, together with his brother, William, was a principal in a firm of naval architects, whose most notable assignment had been the design of the superliner *United States*, the luxurious ship that after an Atlantic crossing that took just three days, ten hours, and forty minutes, returned the *Blue Riband* to the U.S. in 1952.

When not occupied by the draining task of designing ships, Frederick Gibbs spent his time at the estate in Stamford, where he kept a stable of cars. His tastes gravitated towards the fast and racy, but the way in which he regarded them was perhaps a bit eccentric, in that he saw the cars more as objects for the enjoyment of his engineer's mind than for the pleasure of sporty driving.

Before his death in 1978, he had ordered the restoration of the Testa Rossa. On the day of

its completion, the interviewed employee (as retold by him) was present as Gibbs' personal representative, and recalls one of Chinetti's Italian mechanics placing a glass of water on top of the hood. With the engine running, there was not a crease on the water's surface—testimony to the state of tune.

It later fell to the employee to dispose of Gibbs' cars, all of which were bought by a local collector. The Testa Rossa stayed with this owner for a number of years, after which time it was finally sold to a collector in Switzerland.

The Top Ten Testa Rossa today resides in the private collection of a man whose name is very much in the public eye. As a car enthusiast, he therefore prefers anonymity.

The most original Testa Rossa in existence—The Virgin—still lives in seclusion. It is, however, not allowed to gather dust, a fact testified to by its deployment during the photo session, when, for the effect of a speed shot, the exquiste collector piece was run up to a screaming 7000 rpm—at which point, incidentally, local police intervened.

Luckily, no ticket resulted. The cop was a true Ferrari fancier, and the Testa Rossa was certainly one of Enzo's best.

250 GT CALIFORNIA

1960

A Topless Ferrari With Two Lives

The vignette to the right, shows the prototype Spyder California, chassis 0769, under construction in Maranello. Completed on December 16, 1957, the machine was delivered to George Arents. Seen below, our Top Ten feature at the start of the 1960 Le Mans. Sturgis/Schlesser lasted twenty-one hours before being forced to call it quits with engine trouble. In the color picture, opposite, the wider stance of the short-wheelbase Spyder is evident.

It was the year of the U-2 spy plane incident, of Khrushchev banging his shoe at the United Nations, and Kennedy narrowly defeating Nixon to capture the presidential election.

It was the year of the Rome Olympiad, of Rathman winning the Indy 500, and of Patterson becoming the first to regain the heavyweight title.

It was the year 1960.

For the Man in Maranello, the year marked the final season of the front-engined Grand Prix machines, and a poor one at that, producing just one victory. The sports cars yielded some solace, however, scoring a dual win at Le Mans, picking up a third World Championship title in the process.

At the business level, Ferrari could look with satisfaction on an annual production output that had risen to between 300 and 400 automobiles.

On a strictly personal plane, Ferrari—who celebrated his sixty-second birthday on February 18—would not, or, perhaps, was not able to, let go of the grief over his son, Dino, who had died in 1956. The introspection that resulted had taken the form of a self-imposed seclusion that kept Ferrari tied to Maranello, away from the race tracks.

As far as automotive fashion and form was concerned, the year 1960 saw the ripening of the Ferrari style.

On the production side, this look was championed by such timeless designs as the 250 GT Coupe, and the dual-purpose 250 GT SWB (short-wheelbase berlinetta), both, as denoted, closed cars. On the topless level, these two were paralleled by the 250 GT Cabriolet, as well as the virtually dual-purpose 250 GT California.

The Spyder California, which, as it concerned styling, took its cue from the 250 GT Pinin Farina Spyder (built in a very limited run of three dozen cars between 1956 and 1957), was the result of pressure from Luigi Chinetti, who, from his American vantage point, saw real sales potential among the rich and famous out West—a world where the sun never seemed to set.

Sure enough, the beautiful people, with sexy Brigitte Bardot in the lead (she is believed to have bought two), responded as predicted to the temptation of an equipage that so eloquently reflected their image.

Other famous owners were Francoise Sagan, the novelist, and James Coburn, the macho screen hero. Amongst the racing professionals, Josef Siffert and Wolfgang von Trips were known to have transferred their track passion—usually expressed from

At von Trips' funeral, the coffin was conveyed to its final resting place perched atop his prized Spyder California...

behind the wheel of wicked Testa Rossas—to their respective pair of Californias when indulging in road pleasures.

On a tragic note, but as an epilogue befitting an audacious challenger of speed: After von Trips' fatal accident at Monza in 1961, at his funeral, the coffin was conveyed to its final resting place perched atop his prized Spyder California.

Seen from an engineering point of view, the California (the first example of which had received its finishing touches by December 16, 1957), was, as one had come to expect of Ferrari, rather conservative.

Independent rear suspension, although this was used on the Ferrari race cars, had not found its way to the road cars. These still sported stiff axles supported by leaf springs.

The brakes were still of the drum variety and, as learned by many the hard way, no match for the power.

The wheelbase, with its rather long 2600 mm, provided good stability at high speeds although it made the car a bit unwieldy through tight turns.

Power again came from the Colombo engine, which sported the classic stroke dimension of 58.8 mm. The bore was 73 mm, which produced the volume

of 2953 cc. A compression of 9 to 1 and a trio of twin-throat 36DLC/3 Webers produced 240 hp at 7000 rpm. Top speed, when using a 9/33 rear axle ratio, was 150 mph.

The gearbox consisted of a four-speed all-synchromesh unit mounted in conjunction with the engine. It was manufactured in-house at Maranello.

The body was built by Sergio Scaglietti, although its shape was the product of Pinin Farina, whose surname, incidentally, would be changed to Pininfarina in 1961, an honor bestowed on the aging ambassador of Italian coachbuilding art through a presidential decree.

Scaglietti, whose medium had predominantly been that of aluminum, switched to steel for the California, except for the hood, doors and trunk lid, which were of the lighter metal.

Taking its styling cues from the Leopold Ferrari, whose basic theme it had inherited, the California was in fact a topless variation of the *Tour de France* Berlinetta as far as both shape and engineering.

Later, with the advent of the Short-Wheelbase Berlinetta, the Spyder California inherited the mechanical specifications of this shorter machine, although not the styling aspect.

The Spyder California, even though it was fitted with roll-up windows--and thus was further removed from the primitive spyder theme--was the first to actually be listed as a spyder in Ferrari's sales literature. Above, the dashboard of the prototype featured a cluster of gauges, like that in the Tour de France Berlinetta, while--as on our Top Ten car--the gauges later were lined up in a row along the face of the dash. This became standard fare for the Spyder California.

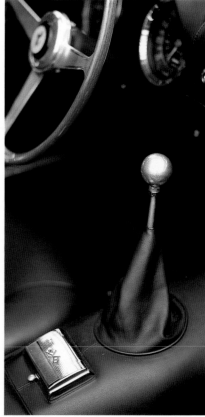

The four-speed gearbox of the Spyder California was operated through a strong, stubby shift lever, topped by a no-nonsense aluminum knob. In the picture to the left, our Top Ten feature car shows off its frontal aspects--both fashionable and ferocious. Covered headlights certainly lent more litheness to the lines. The scoop on the long-wheelbase version, was placed on top of the hood, while--as seen to the left--the short-wheelbase featured it recessed into the hood.

The result was a look that expressed a consummately capable machine. The effect was of massive power rather than, as before, of slim elegance...

This new model, the second generation California, bowed in 1960. It had graduated to both disc brakes and shock absorbers. These features had also been incorporated on the last of the long-wheelbase cars.

Also at this time, with regards to the engine, the spark plugs were moved from inside the vee to the outside and the hairpin valve springs exchanged for coil types. Power had increased to 280 hp at 7000 rpm.

The new and improved model featured a wheelbase that had been cut by as much as 200 mm, which resulted in lower weight and better handling.

The cutting had of course not been limited to the chassis, but had also caused the elimination of 450 mm from the length of the body. The result was a look that expressed massive power rather than, as before, elegance. Later, a widening of the front and rear treads, in addition to a change-over to fifteen-inch rims, provided further magnification of that massive look.

Now, finally separated from the styling of the Tour de France, the short-wheelbase California became its own exclusive model entity—a new breed.

Both the long-wheelbase and the short-wheelbase versions came with covered or uncovered headlights. It is said that the

covered headlight feature was first introduced to the California by Scaglietti—who, as already mentioned, manufactured the bodies—together with a number of minor body alterations.

The choice between covered and uncovered headlights, as far as which solution is the most desirable, should be left to the eye of the beholder, perhaps, but a majority of observers seem to agree that the covered version is the design of choice.

The process of choosing a Top Ten finalist could be compared to the dismantling of a pyramid from the bottom up. In the case of the California, two major choices affected the elimination of two bottom levels. These were, firstly, the choice of the short-wheelbase version (totalling some 55 units) over the long-wheelbase variation (of which 46 were made); secondly, the choice of covered lights over uncovered.

Further limiting was needed, however, and racing history once again played a role in the final selection.

Although the California was indeed built primarily for use on the road, its ancestry was such that track appearances became common. A dozen Spyders left the factory specially set up for this purpose and sported a hot

These black and white photographs illustrate the sleek lines of the long-wheelbase Spyder California. The particular example featured is chassis 1641, the fifth from the end of the run, completed on January 29, 1960. It is one of the dozen Californias with aluminum body and competition engine. As far as known, the machine was never raced during its early days, but has in recent years seen serious action in historic racing.

The Spyder California could handle the part with equal flair whether on the track--especially in lightweight configuration--or in a picturesque postcard setting, as evidenced by this series of photographs of our Top Ten selection at its place of domicile in the Swiss Alps, near the posh ski resort of Gstaad. The only exterior giveaway that this beautiful car is in reality a very potent racing machine--having run at Le Mans--is found in the filler cap, seen in the picture at the top of the previous page.

Although conceived primarily for use on the road, the heritage of the California was such that race track cameos were inevitable...

The faded magazine clipping to the right, shows our Top Ten feature car leading the pack at the start of the 1961 Sebring, where it managed an honorable twelfth overall. At the bottom of this page, the same machine is hidden in the field at the start of one of the two events it competed in during the 1961 Nassau Speed Week. The engine, below and right, was obscured by the cold-air pan, leaving only the velocity stacks visible.

engine, an all-aluminum body, and a larger fuel tank equipped with outside filler cap.

Of these special Californias, only three units were of the short version. And only one of these three had a track history: chassis 2015, which thus became the Top Ten finalist.

Number 2015 was delivered in Cannes—that French Riviera playground of the film fraternity. The date was June 20, 1960, the customer, Jan de Vroom.

This California would not be the toy of a playboy, however. Heading northwest, the machine immediately steered towards a rendezvous with its destiny: the 24 Hours of Le Mans.

Number 2015 sported a Tipo 168B engine under the hood, which meant a unit similar to the ones powering the Testa Rossa. The setup applied special valves, hotter camshafts, and bigger Webers, which added up to the most powerful California ever put on road or track.

With Frenchman Jo Schlesser and American Bill Sturgis at the wheel, 2015 did well during the race, climbing as high as 11th overall. But, with only two hours to go, engine failure forced a regrettable retirement.

After Le Mans, number 2015 was sold to Chinetti, who, after a thorough overhaul, entered the car in the 1961 Sebring.

With Allan Newman, Robert Publicker, and Gaston Andrey sharing the driving chores, the machine managed a 12th.

At the end of the year, 2015 rounded out its racing career by contesting two of the events run during the Nassau Speed Week. In the Governor's Trophy Race, Allan Newman did not finish, while in the main event Nassau Tourist Trophy Race, George Arents managed a 26th.

Today, three decades after its sojourn on the racetrack, and after a long succession of owners—of which John and Bill Gelles were the most faithful, caring for the survivor for well over a decade—2015 finally lives another life, a life among the glamorous people.

Restored to perfection, it is now housed as an invited guest beside other Ferraris of special distinction, all preserved in a bunker-like building hidden in the Swiss Alps near Gstaad—the favorite gathering spot for the international ski set, where once in awhile a red, topless Ferrari can be seen drifting down the main drag, competing for the attention of the Roger Moores and the Elizabeth Taylors of the rich and famous.

These, then, were the dual purposes of a Spyder California: Guts and Glamour.

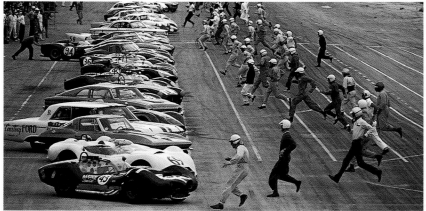

Ferrari Dominate Sebring

1966

365 CALIFORNIA

A Forgotten Ferrari Comes to the Fore

Judging from the miniscule number of photographs that can be found of the 365 California, the model must be one of the most rare--the vignette to the right is one of a series taken when the prototype, chassis 8347, was finished. Our Top Ten feature car, opposite page, number 9615, as it looks today. Below, head of the family to which the car first belonged--feared dictator of the Dominican Republic, Rafael Trujillo-- plays rough with one of his grandsons.

A little more than a decade had passed since the father of the Ferrari style formulated his definitive statement on the matter of the luxury convertible: the Leopold Cabriolet.

Much had occurred since the introduction of that memorable Pininfarina milestone; a grand procession of masterpieces had flowed from the workshops on Via Lesna in Turin and business had been good. Pininfarina was no longer just a builder of low volume sports and racing cars, but had joined the fraternity of industrialists, employing mass-production methods.

Alfa Romeo, Fiat and Lancia were his main customers, but Peugeot and Austin also joined the fray. The hand of the man who had begun his trade at the age of eleven, had emerged to shape all the most important developments in the arena of automotive styling.

Now, in early 1966, however, the time had come for change. The hand of the old Master was no longer at the wheel—Battista Pininfarina had passed away in Lausanne on April 3.

At the time of his passing, another luxury convertible had been on the drawing board. By the end of 1965, the project had progressed to the metal stage, and on January 27 the first unit stood completed.

This big-league 2+2, which was introduced at the Geneva Salon in March, became known as the 365 California. Last of the grand luxury convertibles to emerge from Ferrari, the car could be characterized as the *Forgotten Ferrari.*

As a matter of fact, the 365 California, which was duplicated only fourteen times, seemed to have been passed over already in its infancy: the factory never printed a separate catalog.

The real reason for the low profile that the California produces in the gallery of Ferrari greats should be attributed to the actuality that the model, with its excessive weight, its equally extravagant appearance, and its less-than-outstanding handling characteristics, was never able to generate any passion among the serious Ferrari enthusiasts in the first place.

Today, as the unique qualities of all Ferraris are re-examined, the 365 California finally comes to the fore. This re-evaluation does not shut its eyes to the short-comings of the model; rather it looks beyond them, which results in the discovery of a machine of rare distinction, as well as a re-confirmation of the old adage that demonstrates the idiom: there is always more to a matter than meets the eye.

The most distinctive aspect of the 365 California—in that classic Ferrari tradition—was its engine...

The styling theme for the front of the California came from the Superamerica, with its elongated nose and minimal grille. Our Top Ten car was photographed in England, where this idyllic country setting, a bit mistreated by wear and tear, provides a poignant contrast to the polished surfaces of the beautifully finished California. In true Ferrari tradition, the engraved steering wheel was by Nardi, while the spoke wire wheels were by Borrani.

Perhaps the most distinctive aspect of the unique 365 California—in that classic Ferrari tradition—was its engine.

As installed in the 365, the unit was designated the Tipo 217A. Genetically, the machine originated from the Colombo design which, after twenty years was still going strong. In this configuration, the engine had its roots in the Tipo 209, which was developed for Ferrari's 1962 3967 cc 400 Superamerica, and produced 340 hp.

A second version of the Tipo 209 was developed for use in the 330 GT 2+2, introduced in 1964. At this time, the space between the bore centers had been increased, creating a *long* version of the classic Colombo engine as well.

The third development phase was reached with the 4963 cc 500 Superfast. Rating was now reportedly 400 hp.

The fourth stage was the machine that powered the 365 California. It now produced 320 hp at 6600 rpm. The bore had been increased from 77 mm to 81 mm. The stroke stayed at 71 mm, creating a 4390 cc displacement.

In this form, the engine saw use on the track, although not as part of a factory team. When, for the 1965 season, privateers asked for power to keep up with the 330 P2—featuring a four-cam engine—Ferrari fitted a few of these cars with the 365 single-cam version. As much as 380 horses were extracted at 7300 rpm. Scuderia Filipinetti timed its car doing 190 mph on the Mulsanne straight.

As the power source for the 365 California, the engine was pressed to compete with such performance-draining equipment as air conditioning and power steering. In spite of this, plenty of force was on hand to produce the paragon of touring expected by captains of industry and others with deep pockets.

One such owner, reiterating his experience of commuting from Monte Carlo to Genoa via the curvy coastal road, spoke of effortless cruising in the 90-to-110 mph range, interspersed with bursts of 130 mph on short straightaways. This is the kind of travelling referred to in classic terminology as *rapid motoring in luxurious comfort*.

The fascinating aspect of the 365 California, however, was that the voyage did not have to take place in a boring, sleep-inducing mode. On the contrary, the occupants were entertained with alluring songs of *ripping canvas*, emerging clean, crisp and melodious, emanating from a twin set of big-voiced dual exhaust pipes.

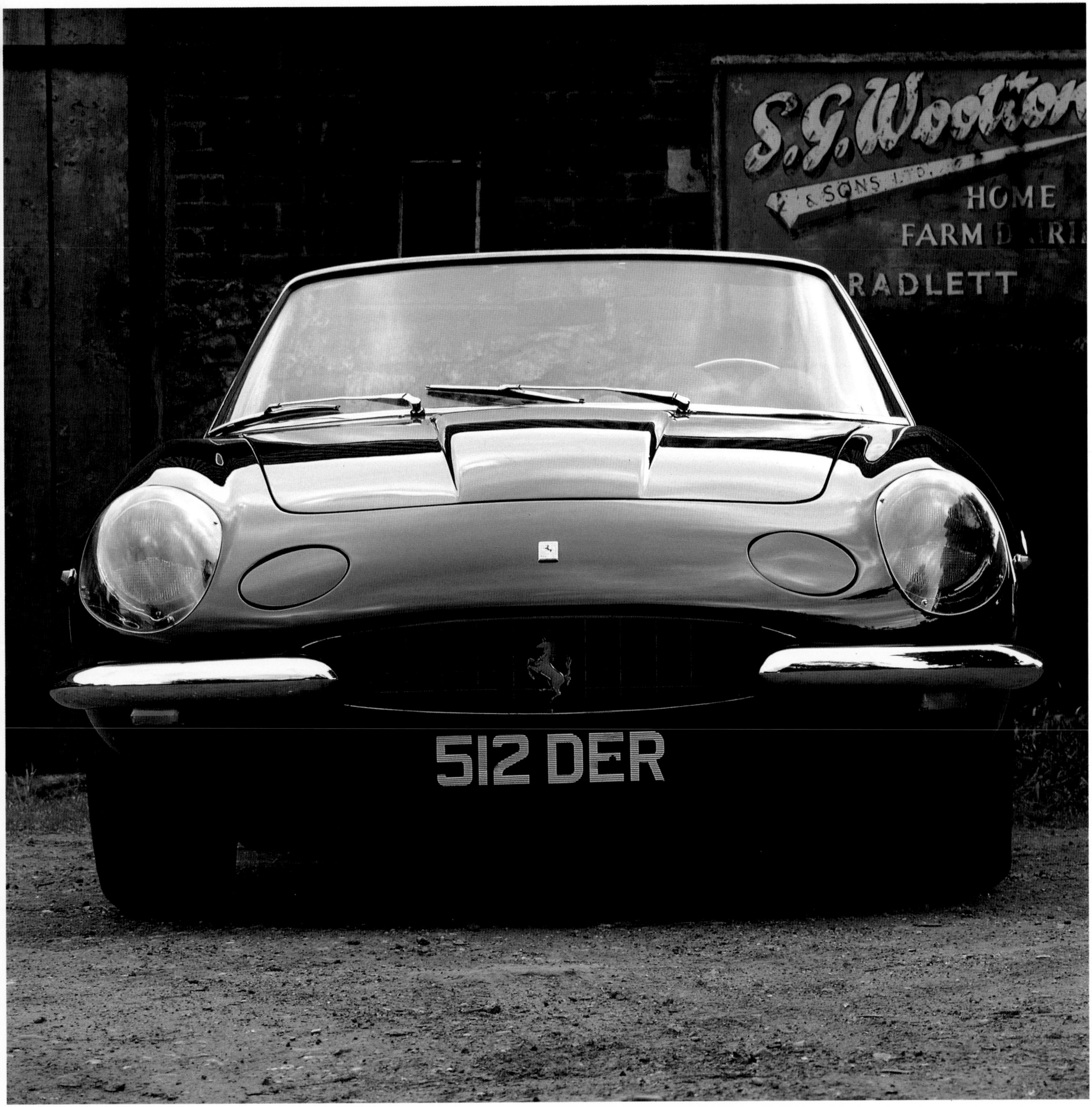
S.G.Woottor
& SONS LTD.
HOME
FARM D IRI
RADLETT
512 DER

The exhaust note emerged crisp, clear and melodious, coming eagerly from a twin set of big-voiced dual exhaust pipes...

Chassiswise, the California displayed conventional fare. Derived from the 330 GT 2+2 and the 500 Superfast, the new model carried on the front and rear suspensions of these—down to the rigid rear axle—as well as the long, 2650 mm wheelbase, making it the longest-ever Ferrari of the topless variety.

With all this metal to carry around (a matter further added to by the voluminous luggage compartment which demanded a massive rear and extensive amounts of steel) overall weight became a problem, with the machine tipping the scale at just under 4000 pounds.

Also a problem, reported by owners, was chassis flexing, which, coupled with the weight at the rear—and aggravated by the rigid rear axle—tended to induce oversteer.

Fortunately, considering the weight, there were disc brakes on all four wheels. The wheels, incidentally, were Borrani wires as standard, with the new cast alloys optional. The gearbox produced five all-synchromesh speeds and was mounted up front with the engine.

The level of craftsmanship was outstanding, as exemplified by the interior and its abundant use of leather and wood.

Stylingwise, the somewhat less than satisfying result could

perhaps be seen as simply the product of the confusing trends characterizing styling at that time, when the mid-engine layout forced the designers to re-think the classic approach.

In the styling of the California, this confusion can perhaps be illustrated by the combination of elements taken from different cars and periods. The front, for instance, was inherited from the Superfast and Superamerica tradition, with its smooth, small-grilled, snout-nosed appearance, which was simple and pleasing. Confusion materialized when an element from Pininfarina's mid-engine Dino show car—the long, concave door handle recess—was introduced. Final damage was done to the rear, which, with its knife-sharp creases and angles, represented a completely new theme—one also found in Pininfarina's contemporary Fiat 124 Spyder—and, in this writer's opinion, a disappointing ending to a promising beginning.

Of the fourteen Californias built, when considering the Top Ten selection, the first and the last units seemed examples of most importance.

Of the remaining cars, a few were found to be in somewhat less than pristine condition. Two had seen their original pop-up foglights removed, and two had

The 365 California was premiered at the 1966 Geneva Salon. Number 10155, was one of three units listing a build date of November 5, 1966. It was shown by Autohaus Becker, the German Ferrari importer, at the 1967 auto show in Frankfurt. The two black and white photographs on the previous page illustrate its appearance at this event. Left and below, our Top Ten car shows off its side and rear views. The latter was not its strongest point.

One of the cars possessed a most intriguing early history—it had first belonged to the Trujillo family, the infamous dictator...

been fitted with non-original accessories such as grille guard and fender-mounted mirrors. One of the cars was undergoing restoration. But, significantly, the exact whereabouts of two of the cars was unknown. This, one must reflect, was of course a fate that could only befall a forgotten Ferrari.

In addition to the first and the last examples, however, there surfaced one perfectly restored car, still surviving in England, one possessing a most intriguing early history: It had first been owned by members of the Trujillo family. These three cars, then, were the Top Ten finalists.

The prototype, supposedly in Belgium, turned out to have no recent address and the last unit built, now in England, proved to be in the hands of an owner more reclusive than Howard Hughes. As a result, just 9615 remained, the proud possession of Robert Beecham.

For over thirty years, Rafael Trujillo headed one of the most oppressive dictatorships in Latin America. Disrespect for human rights and wide-spread corruption finally prompted his assassination in 1961.

Trujillo's son, Rafael, Jr., took over, and soon the family was back playing its old game. U.S. gun-boat diplomacy forced the entire Trujillo family into exile at the end of 1961.

True to form, cash had been stashed in foreign banks. The lifestyle could be continued, and fancy cars were a part of the picture. And this is where 9615 enters the scene.

The silver-gray beauty was delivered on January 30, 1967 in Madrid, Spain, to one of the Trujillo sons. The dictator had a number of male offspring and which individual in particular claimed the keys to the car has not been established.

This leaves the epilogue a bit unclear. It is known, however, that one of the sons met his final destiny when he crashed the Ferrari at high speed.

Robert Beecham has learned some of the subsequent adventures of his California. It was bought from the Trujillo family directly after the accident and had not been repaired. The second owner had the car patched up, while the third gave it a thorough restoration.

Beecham, the fourth owner, puts it first among his collection of Ferraris, prizing the car as the product of the same formula that brought forth the Leopold cabriolet: lavish grand touring luxury combined with awesome power derived directly from a race tested engine.

In contrast to the primitive spyders of the past, when only the most basic needs were catered to, the dash of the 365 had a full luxury complement, including clock, cigar lighter, and radio. Opposite page, upper left, the door featured a design borrowed from a Ferrari show car. Lower left, the power plant was a 320 hp brute, but could hardly be seen under all the hardware. To the left, the engine compartment of the 365 GT 2+2, a sister car.

275 GTS/4 NART

1967

Wildcat Ferrari Turns Into Winner

Commendatore Ferrari was never known to be generous when it came to giving credit. Within his domain—the factory—the cars were forged to *his* mold. They were *his* inventions, and the men who labored there were under the direction and control of *The Agitator of Men*—the term Ferrari often used to describe his own pivotal role.

Outside his domain—on the race tracks—his autocratic bent showed in his bias towards the cars, which were always number one. The drivers were just hired hands. As late as the mid-fifties, team members were paid only four or five hundred dollars per month—the car was the star.

This is not to say that Ferrari was incapable of expressing his appreciation. He did so, but on rare occasions, most publicly in his memoirs, *My Terrible Joys*, where drivers and collaborators were characterized in phrases that often turned out to be more incisive than indulgent.

One name commonly absent, conspicuously so, was that of Luigi Chinetti—the man who almost single-handedly was responsible for giving Ferrari his first and most important international win (Le Mans, 1949), the man who brought The Prancing Horse to the awareness of the New World (Carrera Panamericana, 1951), and the man who broke the

ground in affluent America, cultivating it into Ferrari's most lucrative market.

Perhaps Ferrari and Chinetti were too much alike. They were both agitators, both talented organizers, and both ambitious. Chinetti harbored dreams of building his own race cars, and, although he never came that far, he ran his own racing team, much like Ferrari had done for prewar Alfa Romeo.

In 1966, it was practically a decade since Chinetti had stimulated the conception of the 250 GT California. Now the shrewd marketeer pushed a new idea: another spyder. This time, however, the Commendatore would not cooperate.

What emerged was a wildcat Ferrari, a unique species, one that through the years advanced to the front row among those all-time most-sought-after, yet one that was never recognized by the Ferrari factory.

Chinetti certainly had good reasons for his request. In the mid-sixties, Ferrari's production car line had been divided into four branches: one, the luxurious 500 Superfast; two, the four-seater 330 GT; three, the potent 275 GTB; and four, the vapid 275 GTS—the only topless model in the lineup, and one that with its detuned engine and sober

A 1967 program cover provides the lead-in to the coverage of our Top Ten car, which raced at Sebring that year. On the previous page, the Spyder at speed, with Denise McCluggage doing the driving. Pictured at the bottom of the page, the Spyder tries to keep up with the Hall/Spence Chaparral. Left, at one point, the car ran first in class, which prompted the pit crew to deploy the plywood floor from the trunk of the Spyder as message board.

Having failed, for reasons unknown, to gain Ferrari's cooperation, Chinetti went straight to Scaglietti...

styling, projected a decidedly bourgeois image. Chinetti, and many loyal supporters of the true sporting tradition, craved a machine that expressed both power and pizzazz.

Having failed, for reasons unknown, to obtain Ferrari's constructive response, Chinetti went straight to Scaglietti, whose carrozzeria built the bodies for the 275 GTB. A deal was struck between the two, which called for the manufacture of twenty-five spyders, based on the 275 GTB. They would be marketed solely in North America and be distributed exclusively through Chinetti Motors, established in Greenwich, Connecticut.

The first NART (so named for the initials of Chinetti's North American Racing Team) Spyder appeared in New York during February 1967. Stamped with chassis number 09437, the car sported a pale yellow paint job and was built to the order of a certain Peter Brunt.

The second NART, 09751, arrived in March. Sporting a fly yellow skin matched by black seats, it went to Stamford resident Alfred Goldschmidt.

The third car, 10139, arrived in July. It was orange, with an orange interior, and became the property of John McGeary, of Miami, Florida.

The fourth NART Spyder to be built, chassis 10219, arrived in August. The car repeated the yellow and black color scheme and went to Chicago resident Benjamin Gould.

These four cars are thought to have been built from scratch, using the GTB panels, while the six subsequent Spyders seem to have been created through a modification process—a belief nurtured by the fact that original invoices for these cars show a surcharge for *Modification from Berlinetta to Spyder.* All of the cars, however, are attributed to Carrozzeria Scaglietti.

When it came to narrowing the choice for a Top Ten candidate, it seemed one of the first four should have an edge. The very first unit, which most often seems to take on a special significance, advanced to the front, especially so when it was found that it had both a racing and a movie career, although the latter was more brief than the former—to the tune of twelve hours, compared to, shall we say, twelve seconds.

Peter Brunt, to whose order the prototype car had been built, apparently never took delivery. Chinetti instead decided to give his offspring some exposure and entered it in the 12-Hours of Sebring, run on April 1.

Despite the fact that the Ferrari factory did not recognize the NART as a regular catalog model, Ferrari Public Relations supplied the motoring press with the photograph shown at the bottom of the previous page. Denise McCluggage, in the scene above, gets ready to race. The front and rear views, illustrate the full-bodied forms of Pininfarina's design--one some thought a bit too round. Nevertheless, the 275 GTB illustrates the last of the classic Ferrari style.

McCluggage kept the Spyder in the lead until, during a tire change, the disorganized pit crew lost one of the wheels—and ten minutes...

Chinetti selected two women to co-drive his NART Spyder at Sebring: Denise McCluggage, the gutsy automotive journalist, and Pinkie Rollo, a pert redhead with a competition background in show-horse jumping. The pair could point to previous racing adventures. McCluggage, among other feats, had driven a Ferrari Berlinetta to a class win and an impressive tenth position overall in the 1961 Sebring.

A few years earlier, the two had teamed up in an OSCA, also at Sebring, and were therefore, if not seasoned veterans, without question well-qualified for the choice assignment.

Luigi Chinetti had this year been forced to remain at home, fearing legal trouble resulting from a fatal accident involving a NART-team Ferrari during the previous year's race. His absence manifested itself most clearly in an unfortunate lack of pit-crew organization.

The Spyder started out well and soon established itself as the leader in its category, Class 12 Grand Touring, with the closest competitor a Shelby.

The lead held until, during a tire change, the pit-crew was unable to locate the fourth wheel. Ten minutes were lost, and by the time the Ferrari was back on track the Shelby had taken a commanding lead.

Thanks to some enterprising driving during the dark hours, when McCluggage's sharp *red-shift* night vision gave her an edge, the pale-yellow NART, by the time the twelve hours were up, was on the same lap as the Shelby and just a few short seconds down.

Managing a fine seventeenth overall, the NART turned out to be the single Ferrari survivor among a field that had included seven at the start.

After the race, the prototype Spyder went back to Chinetti for an all-inclusive overhaul and a paint job—burgundy this time. Properly refurbished, 09437 was turned over to *Road & Track* for a road test, an article appearing in the September issue.

After the test session, Chinetti licensed the prototype Spyder to the producers of *The Thomas Crown Affair,* a 1968 movie thriller starring Faye Dunaway and dyed-in-the-wool sports car enthusiast Steve McQueen, who procured a Spyder of his own, number 10453.

Mechanically, the Spyder, and therefore also the 275 GTB/4, which formed the basis for the topless car, constituted the most advanced Ferrari road machine up to this point.

Consider the following list of choice specifications: All-around

The two illustrations at the top of the previous page--snapped by a Scaglietti visitor in 1967--are, despite their poor quality, of extreme interest, as they establish the only known photographic links between the coachbuilder and the NART Spyder. The shot of the clay model raises more questions than it answers, however. Was it created by Pininfarina to be used as a pattern by the coachbuilder, or was it made by Scaglietti independently?

Zero to sixty took six point seven seconds, the quarter mile fourteen point seven—figures that prompted the veteran tester to exclaim: Ah, ecstacy!

A Road & Track photographer snapped these black and white shots for the magazine's 1967 road test of our Top Ten feature car. The side view on the previous page was taken at the same occasion and shows future Road & Track editor Tony Hogg during a stint behind the wheel. The interior was identical to that of the 275 GTB/4, as was the engine. Four overhead cams, and six twin-throat carburetors gave more than ample power.

independent suspension, a most welcome addition that Ferrari enthusiasts had been waiting for with patience. Spelled out, the front and rear designs read the same: unequal A-arms joined by coil springs, tube shocks, and roll-bar. Rear-mounted gear box, another feature that had been long in coming; five-speed, all-synchromesh transmission; disc brakes—sporting a swept area expansive enough to match the power: 493 square inches; an engine with four overhead cams, six Weber carburetors, and a power output of as much as 330 hp at 8000 rpm—the bore and stroke measured 77 mm by 58.8 mm, which gave a 3286 cc displacement.

The thorough *Road&Track* tryout produced an intriguing set of acceleration figures: zero to 60 mph took 6.7 seconds, while the quarter-mile was covered in just 14.7 seconds. Top speed was 155 mph—data that prompted the seasoned writer to sigh with pleasure: *Ah, ecstacy!*

After its successful sojourn at Sebring and its brief but blissful rendezvous with Thomas Crown, our Top Ten choice was returned to Chinetti's showroom, from where it was purchased by Norman Silver of High Point, North Carolina, who kept the car until his death a few years

ago. At this point, the priceless survivor came to the attention of Don Andrews, of Shelton Ferrari, Fort Lauderdale, Florida, who subsequently contacted Dano Davis, a longtime Ferrari enthusiast living in Jacksonville, Florida. This encounter led to Davis purchasing the car and Andrews supervising a first-class restoration that put the Spyder back in its original condition, down to its pale yellow—*Giallo Solare*, as it so sensuously is referred to in the language of the coachbuilder.

And now to the credits: Enzo Ferrari, of course—The Great Agitator of Men; Colombo and Lampredi—the pioneers; Carlo Chiti—who picked up where they left off; Mauro Forghieri, Franco Rocchi and Giancarlo Bussi—the *Troika* directly responsible for the engineering of the period; Sergio Pininfarina—the son who took over from his father; Sergio Scaglietti—the master of metal manipulation; Luigi Chinetti—the man from whose bright vision the Spyder sprung. It was a vision that produced one of the most powerful and beautiful Ferraris ever to hit the road.

Only in one respect did Chinetti's vision for the Spyder fall short—just ten were built. But this, in the final analysis, only makes the car that much more unique and desirable.

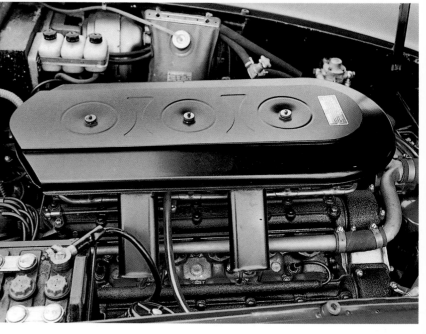

1969

365 GTS/4 DAYTONA

First of the Last of the Line

A student of Ferrari production data may understandably react with confusion at the sight of the model year listed in the subtitle at the top of the page—he would know that the Daytona Spyder did not become available until during 1971.

What he may not be aware of, however, is that the prototype Daytona Spyder was actually completed during the autumn of 1969, and was first exhibited at the Frankfurt show in October of that same year.

What this means, then, is that our Top Ten selection must be the prototype—which it indeed is; chassis number 12851.

The Daytona Spyder was the topless representation of the Daytona Berlinetta, a model first exhibited during the 1968 Paris Salon. Its authorized model designation was 365 GTB/4. The catchy Daytona appellation, although thought to have been used by Ferrari engineers during the production phase, was not official, but was pushed publicly by the cheering motoring press, ostensibly in honor of Ferrari's triple victory at the 1967 24-Hour race at Daytona.

The Daytona was faster than any other road car Ferrari had built until then. At the time, it was also the fastest production car on the road—a French magazine

pitted it against a Lamborghini Miura and three other super-car competitors, with the Ferrari coming out on top, recording a top speed of 172 mph to 169 mph for the Miura. The factory listed a top speed of 174 mph. Perhaps the objective figure lay right in between, as *Road & Track* recorded 173 mph during its test. Zero to sixty took 5.9 seconds, while 100 mph came up 6.1 seconds later.

A provenance of even more provocation to the test team was the experience of shifting from fourth to fifth gear at a 148 mph speedometer reading!

Behind all this soul-stirring performance was an engine of outstanding sophistication. The machine had most recently been providing power for Ferrari's two and four-seat coupes of the mid-sixties, but its use in the Daytona had been preceded by extensive development.

In the tradition of the 275 GTB/4, the revised engine had also received four overhead camshafts, as well as dry sump lubrication. The cylinder heads used hemispherical combustion chambers, and breathing was through six twin-throat Webers—a doubling of the capacity as compared to the former version. Power produced by the 4390 cc volume engine had surged to 352 hp at 7500 rpm.

The styling of the Daytona was right on the mark, projecting modern lines without moving too far from the familiar sports car concept...

The prototype Daytona Spyder is the subject of all four photographs on this spread. At the bottom of this page, it is seen displayed at the Frankfurt auto show in 1969. To the right, the car is photographed in Maranello where it, for reasons unknown, remained until 1972. Later it was repainted and lost its original lights. The color views depict the prototype straight from a restoration that put the survivor back to its correct configuration.

The Daytona chassis carried on a proven Ferrari tradition: a construction of oval tubes formed the frame, while the all-around independent suspension featured the familiar coil springs, tubular shock absorbers, and anti-roll bars both front and back. Brakes were four-wheel Dunlop discs, while the transmission consisted of a five-speed unit, attached to the differential.

The wheelbase had the now classic Berlinetta measurement of 2400 mm. The wheels were of a new star motif design, lifted directly from the Grand Prix racing machines.

Unfortunately, especially as it affected the U.S. version—with all the gear required for smog certification—the Daytona turned out too heavy: 2645 pounds, according to some early factory figures, but in reality well over the 3500 mark.

Styling, on the other hand, was right on the mark. It projected modern lines without moving too far away from the traditional concept.

Perhaps the only aspect that caused lamentation in the minds of the enthusiasts was that the Daytona had lost the traditional shape of the grille. This was, of course, necessitated by the need to keep the frontal aspect low and aerodynamically lean.

The styling was once again a pure Pininfarina affair, with the prototype also built by the Turin firm, while production bodies were built by the Scaglietti firm, located in Modena.

When it came time to build the new spyder prototype, however, the assignment was entrusted to Scaglietti, although the styling is said to have been executed by Pininfarina.

As a spyder, the Daytona became, if possible, even more attractive. There was nothing to indicate that the machine had not been intended as a spyder, stylingwise. In fact, the harmony between the broad, diagonal front and the flat, cut-off rear was exceptionally pleasing. So was the styling of the top.

Weightwise, there was little change, although one would have thought that the elimination of the glass would have saved some pounds. Unfortunately, the weight of the top mechanism compensated for this.

As with the berlinetta, hood, doors, and trunk lid were made from aluminum, while the rest of the body was steel.

For its conversion to a topless configuration, the spyder had to be reinforced. The frame was strengthened through the use of heavier tubing for a member that ran along the lower edge,

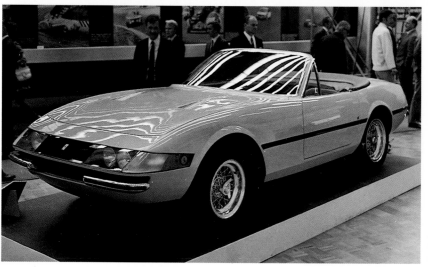

It turned up in Newport Beach in 1977, when its owner—an Iranian Prince—crashed it badly...

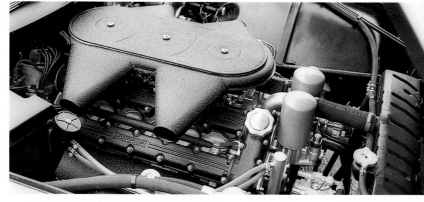

below each door. Under the hood, a brace running down the center of the inner fender panel had tripled in width. Also, the inner fender panels, instead of being built out of fiberglass as on the berlinetta, were changed to steel. It all, of course, served to prevent flexing.

Otherwise, the spyder was in all respects a duplicate of the berlinetta, except when it came to smaller details such as the seatbacks not reclining as much, and the rear window defroster switch being eliminated, certainly for obvious reasons.

The prototype Spyder, after having completed its tour of duty at the Frankfurt Auto Show— where it incidentally had been displayed under the auspices of Autohaus Becker, the German Ferrari agency—was returned to the factory.

Curiously enough, it remained there until 1972, perhaps as a pattern to be activated when the production would begin, which finally happened, starting in the early part of 1971, with some of the first deliveries consisting of right-hand drive cars for the U.K. The first U.S. deliveries came during the summer.

The prototype is thought to have been sold in Europe, as it featured the plexiglass headlight configuration, which was illegal in the U.S. This was the only spyder to feature this design as, by the time the production car arrived, the headlights had been changed to the pop-up version used on both berlinettas and spyders from then on.

Exactly how the prototype made its way to the U.S. is not clear. Regardless, it turned up in Newport Beach, California, in 1977, when its owner at the time—an Iranian prince—crashed it badly. It was repaired, but it is unclear if the conversion to the pop-up version headlights was done at the same time (the damage was to the front end) or if the change had been done in connection with the machine being certified for importation to the United States.

One thing is certain. When Andrew Cohen, owner of Beverly Hills Motoring Accessories—and a Ferrari connoisseur of the first order—bought the car through an ad in the Los Angeles Times, the machine sported the pop-up headlights, and the new owner therefore suspected nothing of its intriguing history.

Another aspect covering the car's past, literally, was the paint job, which was now red. Bright yellow had been the original complexion of the car as shown in Frankfurt.

Cohen first realized that there was something odd about the

The Daytona marked the first move away from the classic Ferrari style. The trend is evident in its broad hood--an area that lost all traces of the fenders of the past. The clarity of the design would certainly have been compromised by the early suggestion of headlights for the American market, seen to the left. Far left, the engine compartment of the 1968 Berlinetta prototype. At the bottom of the previous page, a peek at the Spyder engine compartment.

It was the end of a line that had begun exactly two decades earlier with the introduction of that first little topless Ferrari...

serial number when he made the acquaintance of another owner, whose Spyder—14383—was the first imported to the U.S. Final verification that 12851 was in fact the prototype, came after a call to historian Gerald Roush of the *Ferrari Market Letter.*

This development was indeed a lucky break, and it could not have been bestowed on a more deserving enthusiast, for Cohen never bought any of his cars for speculation, but always for the appreciation of the machine as such. That his Spyder has now suddenly shot to the top of the ladder intrigues him, but only as it pertains to its history.

Cohen, immediately after the purchase, decided to repaint the Spyder black. He drove it like that until 1985, when he began to visualize it in its original state. He contracted Mike Regalia, who, with painstaking accuracy, rebuilt the front end. All the bracing for the Plexiglas lights had to be duplicated from an early berlinetta. The cover itself proved difficult to duplicate. Luckily, a brand new spare was found. Regalia also did the painting, while the interior was done by Tony Nancy.

Altogether, the total number of Daytona Spyders built came to 124. Of these, 96 were of U.S. specification—which in fact illustrates where the Spyder

found its real market—while the remaining 28 were European. Of these, seven examples were built with right-hand drive.

The Daytona Spyder became indeed the last of the real topless Ferraris. With its demise in 1973, also gone was the true Ferrari configuration, the one that demanded the services of a V-12 engine, and the one that called for the power plant to be placed up front.

It was the end of a line whose beginning had been set down exactly two decades earlier, with the creation of the first topless Ferrari—chassis 011—which was fitted with a cabriolet body by Stabilimenti Farina.

In a sense, a new era had begun in 1969, the year Ferrari signed away the production end of his company in a deal with Fiat. Competition was mounting. With mid-engine machines like the Lamborghini on the prowl, Ferrari had to conform. A new line of road machines had to be conceived. Money had to be made. The production line had to be kept moving.

Surely the Commendatore himself, like today's admirers of the classic Ferrari sports cars, must also have missed the good old days when the cars were straightforward and the roads still wide open.

Evidence of the new styling philosophy that characterized the Daytona was perhaps nowhere else as obvious as in the headlight design. Gone were the two separate units that since the days of the classics had been such distinctive focusing points. Although still visible, they were covered by a horizontal strip of Plexiglas--decorated with a pattern of white stripes, no less. The classic badge had not been tampered with, but so radical was the design that a hole had to be cut to allow it to show.

With radical new themes distinguishing the exterior of the Daytona, it was natural that the interior had to follow suit. Here the Pininfarina stylists had come up with a fancy seat design, and a console that, although it kept the shift gate idea, featured the radio set longitudinally. The arrangement of the gauges still followed the classic pattern, with an elliptical pod. It was all very functional, as racing ace Chris Amon had the pleasure of sampling.

Designer: Aurelio Lampredi.
Configuration: V-12...

1949/166 MM Barchetta

Engine
Designer: Gioachino Colombo.
Configuration: Sixty degree,
V-12, water-cooled.
Bore, stroke: 60 mm by 58.8.
Displacement: 1995 cc.
Cylinder block: Light alloy, cast
iron cylinder liners.
Cylinder heads: Two, light alloy,
detachable, siamesed ports.
Valves: Two per cylinder.
Valve actuation: One overhead
camshaft per bank, roller
chain, hairpin springs.
Pistons: Alloy, lightly domed.
Crankshaft: Running in seven
main bearings.
Lubrication: Gear-type pump.
Electrical system: Dual
Marelli magnetos, one spark
plug per cylinder.
Compression ratio: 10 to1.
Carburetion: Three downdraft,
twin-choke Weber 32 DCF.
Power: 140 hp at 6600 rpm.

Drive train
Transmission: Front-mounted
in unit with engine, five-speed,
synchromesh between third
and fourth gears.
Clutch: Single, dry–plate type.
Final drive: Open shaft.

Chassis
Wheelbase: 2200 mm.
Frame: Welded steel tubes.

Front suspension: Independent,
double wishbones, transverse
leaf spring, Houdaille lever-
action shock absorbers.
Rear suspension: Rigid axle,
semi-elliptic springs, Houdaille
lever-action shock absorbers.
Steering: Worm and sector.
Brakes: Hydraulic, aluminum
drums with iron liners.
Wheels: 15-inch, Borrani wire,
center–lock, knock-off.
Tires: 5.50 front and rear.

General
Styling: Carlo Anderloni.
Coachbuilder: Touring, Milan.
Number produced: 19.
Period built: December 1948 to
August 1953.
Dimensions: Overall length,
142.5 inches, width 62 inches,
height 36.5 inches.
Weight: 1470 pounds.
Fuel tank capacity: 26 gallons.
Fuel consumption: 12 mpg.
Zero to 60 mph: 10 seconds.
Top speed: 135 mph.
Bottom line: $16,000 (as fitted
for Chinetti and Lucas).

1951/212 Export

Engine
Designer: Gioachino Colombo.
Configuration: Sixty degree,
V-12, water-cooled.
Bore, stroke: 68 mm by 58.8.
Displacement: 2562 cc.
Cylinder block: Light alloy, cast
iron cylinder liners.
Cylinder heads: Two, light alloy,
detachable.
Valves: Two per cylinder.
Valve actuation: One overhead
camshaft per bank, roller
chain, hairpin springs.
Pistons: Alloy, lightly domed.
Crankshaft: Running in seven
main bearings.
Lubrication: Gear-type pump.
Electrical system: Dual
Marelli magnetos, one spark
plug per cylinder.
Compression ratio: 8 to1.
Carburetion: Three downdraft,
twin-choke Weber 36 DCF.
Power: 170 hp at 6500 rpm

Drive train
Transmission: Front-mounted
in unit with engine, five-speed,
synchromesh between third
and fourth gears.
Clutch: Single, dry–plate type.
Final drive: Open shaft.

Chassis
Wheelbase: 2250 mm.
Frame: Welded steel tubes.

Front suspension: Independent,
double wishbones, transverse
leaf spring, Houdaille lever-
action shock absorbers.
Rear suspension: Rigid axle,
semi-elliptical springs, parallel
trailing arms, Houdaille lever-
action shock absorbers.
Steering: Worm and sector.
Brakes: Hydraulic, aluminum
drums with iron liners.
Wheels: 15-inch, Borrani wire,
center-lock, knock-off.
Tires: 5.90 front and rear.

General
Styling: Giovanni Michelotti.
Coachbuilder: Vignale, Turin.
Number produced: 2.
Date manufactured: Spring 1951.
Dimensions: Overall length,
146.5 inches, width 61.5
inches, height 42.5 inches (with
windshield).
Weight: 2035 pounds.
Fuel tank capacity: 32 gallons.
Fuel consumption: 13 mpg.
Zero to 60 mph: Approximately
7 seconds.
Top speed: About 140 mph.
Bottom line: Not available.

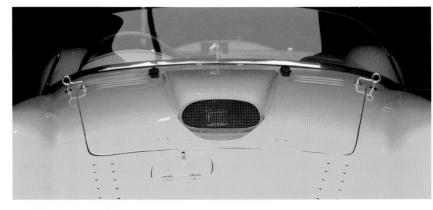

1952/375 Mexico

Engine

Designer: Aurelio Lampredi.
Configuration: Sixty degree, V-12, water-cooled.
Bore, stroke: 80 mm by 68 mm.
Displacement: 4101 cc.
Cylinder block: Light alloy.
Cylinder heads: Two, light alloy, screwed-in liners.
Valves: Two per cylinder.
Valve actuation: One overhead camshaft per bank, chain, hairpin valve springs.
Pistons: Alloy, steeply domed.
Crankshaft: Running in seven thin-wall bearings.
Lubrication: Gear-type.
Electrical system: Twin Marelli magnetos, one spark plug per cylinder.
Compression ratio: 8 to1.
Carburetion: Three downdraft, twin-choke Weber 40 DCF 3.
Power: 280 hp at 6600 rpm.

Drive train

Transmission: Front-mounted in unit with engine, non-synchromesh, five-speed.
Clutch: Multiple, dry-disc type.
Final drive: Open shaft.

Chassis

Wheelbase: 2500 mm.
Frame: Multitubular, welded, elliptical main tubes, rectangular box members.

Front suspension: Independent, double wishbones, transverse leaf spring, rubber blocks, Houdaille lever-action shock absorbers.
Rear suspension: Rigid axle, semi-elliptic springs, four radius rods, Houdaille lever-action shock absorbers.
Steering: Screw and sector.
Brakes: Hydraulic, aluminum drums with iron liners, twin master cylinders.
Wheels: 16-inch, Borrani wire, center-lock, knock-offs.
Tires: 6.00 front, 6.50 rear.

General

Styling: Giovanni Michelotti.
Coachbuilder: Vignale, Turin.
Number produced: 1.
Date manufactured: June 1952.
Dimensions: Overall length, 165.5 inches, width 59 inches, height not available.
Weight: About 2200 pounds.
Fuel tank capacity: 42 gallons.
Fuel consumption: 9.5 mpg.
Zero to 60 mph: Not available.
Top speed: 175mph.
Bottom line: $14,500.

1954/375 Mille Miglia

Engine

Designer: Aurelio Lampredi.
Configuration: Sixty degree, V-12, water-cooled.
Bore, stroke: 84 mm by 68 mm.
Displacement: 4522 cc.
Cylinder block: Light alloy.
Cylinder heads: Two, light alloy, screwed-in liners.
Valves: Two per cylinder.
Valve actuation: One overhead camshaft per bank, chain, hairpin valve springs.
Pistons: Alloy, steeply domed.
Crankshaft: Running in seven thin-wall bearings.
Lubrication: Gear-type.
Electrical system: Dual Marelli magnetos, one spark plug per cylinder.
Compression ratio: 9 to1.
Carburetion: Three downdraft, four-choke Weber 40 IF/4C.
Power: 340 hp at 7000 rpm

Drive train

Transmission: Front-mounted in unit with engine, four-speed, all-synchromesh.
Clutch: Multiple, dry-disc.
Final drive: Open shaft.

Chassis

Wheelbase: 2600 mm.
Frame: Elliptical section, welded steel tubes.

Front suspension: Independent, double wishbones, transverse leaf spring, Houdaille lever-action shock absorbers.
Rear suspension: Rigid axle, semi-elliptical springs, parallel trailing arms, Houdaille lever-action shock absorbers.
Steering: Worm and sector.
Brakes: Hydraulic, aluminum drums with iron liners, two master cylinders.
Wheels: 16-inch, Borrani wire, center-lock, knock-offs.
Tires: 6.00 front, 7.00 rear.

General

Styling: Pinin Farina
Coachbuilder: Pinin Farina.
Number produced: 22.
Period built: September 1953 to September 1954.
Dimensions: Overall length, 165 inches, width 64.5 inches, height 43 inches (includes windshield).
Weight: 2025 pounds.
Fuel tank capacity: 42 gallons.
Fuel consumption: Not available.
Zero to 60 mph: In the 5 second range.
Top speed: About 180 mph.
Bottom line: Not available.

1955/375 Plus Speciale

Engine

Designer: Aurelio Lampredi.
Configuration: Sixty degree, V-12, water-cooled.
Bore, stroke: 84 mm by 74.5 mm.
Displacement: 4954 cc.
Cylinder block: Light alloy.
Cylinder heads: Two, light alloy, screwed-in liners.
Valves: Two per cylinder.
Valve actuation: One overhead camshaft per bank, chain, hairpin valve springs.
Pistons: Alloy, steeply domed.
Crankshaft: Running in seven thin-wall bearings.
Lubrication: Wet sump.
Electrical system: Twin Marelli magnetos, one spark plug per cylinder.
Compression ratio: 8.8 to1.
Carburetion: Three downdraft, twin-choke Weber 42 DCZ.
Power: 344 hp at 6500 rpm.

Drive train

Transmission: Front-mounted in unit with engine, all-synchromesh, four-speed.
Clutch: Dry, multiple disc type.
Final drive: Open shaft.

Chassis

Wheelbase: 2600 mm.
Frame: Welded steel tubes.

Front suspension: Independent, double wishbones, coil springs, Houdaille lever-action shock absorbers.
Rear suspension: Rigid axle, semi-elliptical springs, four locating rods, four Houdaille shock absorbers.
Steering: Independent links.
Brakes: Hydraulic, finned aluminum drums with iron liners, twin master cylinders.
Wheels: 16-inch, Borrani wire, center-lock, three-wing.
Tires: 6.70 front and rear.

General

Styling: Pinin Farina.
Coachbuilder: Pinin Farina.
Number produced: 1.
Date completed: January 1955.
Dimensions: Overall length, 165.5 inches, width 59 inches, height not available.
Weight: About 2900 pounds.
Fuel tank capacity: About 30 gallons.
Fuel consumption: 10 mpg.
Zero to 60 mph: In the low 5-second range.
Top speed: About 170 mph.
Bottom line: $17,000.

1958/250 Testa Rossa

Engine

Designer: Gioachino Colombo, developed by Carlo Chiti.
Configuration: Sixty degree, V-12, water-cooled.
Bore, stroke: 73 mm by 58.8.
Displacement: 2953 cc.
Cylinder block: Light alloy.
Cylinder heads: Two, light alloy, detachable, six ports in each.
Valves: Two per cylinder.
Valve actuation: One overhead camshaft per bank, roller chain, hairpin valve springs.
Pistons: Alloy, BORGO.
Crankshaft: Running in seven thin-walll bearings.
Lubrication: Oil cooler.
Electrical system: Four coils, two distributors, one spark plug per cylinder, located on the outside of the vee.
Compression ratio: 9 to 1.
Carburetion: Six downdraft, twin-choke Weber 38 DCN/6.
Power: 300 hp at 7200 rpm.

Drive train

Transmission: Front-mounted in unit with engine, four-speed all-synchromesh.
Clutch: Single disc, dry-plate.
Final drive: Open shaft.

Chassis

Wheelbase: 2350 mm.
Frame: Welded multitube structure (190 pounds).
Front suspension: Independent, double wishbones, coil springs, Houdaille lever-action shock absorbers.
Rear suspension: Rigid axle, semi-elliptical springs, parallel trailing arms, Houdaille shock absorbers.
Steering: Worm and sector.
Brakes: Hydraulic, aluminum drums with iron liners.
Wheels: 16-inch, Borrani wire, center-lock, knock-offs.
Tires: 5.50 front, 6.00 rear.

General

Styling: Sergio Scaglietti.
Coachbuilder: Scaglietti.
Number produced: 19.
Period built: November 1957 to July 1958.
Dimensions: Overall length, 162.5 inches, width 65 inches, height 38 inches (includes windshield).
Weight: 1760 pounds.
Fuel tank capacity: 37 gallons.
Fuel consumption: 9 mpg.
Zero to 60 mph: In the 5-second range.
Top speed: About 170 mph.
Bottom line: $11,800.

1960/250 GT Spyder California

Engine
Designer: Gioachino Colombo, developed by Carlo Chiti.
Configuration: Sixty degree, V-12, water-cooled.
Bore, stroke: 73 mm by 58.8.
Displacement: 2953 cc.
Cylinder block: Alloy, outside spark plugs, forced-in liners.
Cylinder heads: Two, light alloy, detachable.
Valves: Two per cylinder, double coil springs.
Valve actuation: One overhead camshaft per bank, chain.
Pistons: Light alloy, BORGO.
Crankshaft: Running in seven thin-wall bearings.
Lubrication: Geared pump.
Electrical system: Two Marelli distributors, one spark plug per cylinder.
Compression ratio: 9.5 to1.*
Carburetion: Three downdraft, twin-choke Weber 42 DCL6.*
Power: 280 hp at 7000 rpm.

Drive train
Transmission: Front-mounted in unit with engine, all-synchromesh, four-speed.
Clutch: Single, dry-plate.
Final drive: Open shaft, limited-slip differential.*

Chassis
Wheelbase: 2400 mm.

Frame: Welded tubular steel.
Front suspension: Independent, double wishbones, coil springs, oleo-dynamic shock absorbers, adjustable.
Rear suspension: Rigid axle, semi-elliptical springs, parallel trailing arms, oleo-dynamic shock absorbers, adjustable.
Steering: Independent links.
Brakes: Four-wheel discs.
Wheels: 15-inch, Borrani wire, center-lock, knock-offs.
Tires: 185x15 all around.

General
Styling: Pinin Farina.
Coachbuilder: Scaglietti.
Number produced: 55 (short-wheelbase version).
Period built: May 1960 to February 1963.
Dimensions: Overall length, 166.5 inches, width 65 inches, height not available.
Weight: About 2100 pounds.*
Fuel tank capacity: 32 gallons.*
Fuel consumption: 15 mpg.*
Zero to 60 mph: In the 5-second range.*
Top speed: 155 mph.*
Bottom line: About $16,000.

*Applies to the featured competition model.

1966/365 California

Engine
Designer: Aurelio Lampredi, developed by Mauro Forghieri.
Configuration: Sixty degree, V-12, water-cooled.
Bore, stroke: 81 mm by 71 mm.
Displacement: 4390 cc.
Cylinder block: Light alloy.
Cylinder heads: Two, light alloy, detachable, shrunk-in liners, hemispherical chambers.
Valves: Two per cylinder, double coil springs.
Valve actuation: One overhead camshaft per bank, chain.
Pistons: Light alloy.
Crankshaft: Running in seven thin-wall bearings.
Lubrication:Gear pump.
Electrical system: Twin coils and distributors, one spark plug per cylinder.
Compression ratio: 8.8 to1.
Carburetion: Three downdraft, twin-choke Weber 40 DFI.
Power: 320 hp at 6600 rpm.

Drive train
Transmission: Up front in unit with engine, five-speed, all-synchromesh.
Clutch: Single dry-plate.
Final drive: Open shaft, limited slip differential.

Chassis
Wheelbase: 2650 mm.

Frame: Welded steel tubes.
Front suspension: Independent, double wishbones, coil springs, telescopic shock absorbers.
Rear suspension: Rigid axle, semi-elliptical leaf springs, parallel trailing arms, location rods, hydraulic shock absorbers.
Steering: Worm and sector, with servo-assist.
Brakes: Four-wheel disc brakes, tandem master cylinders.
Wheels: 15-inch, Borrani wire, center-lock, knock-off.
Tires: 205x15 all around.

General
Styling: Pininfarina.
Coachbuilder: Pininfarina.
Number produced: 14.
Period built: January 1966 to November 1967.
Dimensions: Overall length, 194 inches, width 70 inches, height 51 inches.
Weight: About 2900 pounds (factory figure).
Fuel tank capacity: 26 gallons.
Fuel consumtion: 13 mpg.
Zero to 60 mph: Not available.
Top speed: About 150 mph.
Bottom line: $25,000.

1967/275 GTS/4 NART Spyder

Engine

Designer: Gioachino Colombo, developed by Mauro Forghieri.
Configuration: Sixty degree, V-12, water-cooled.
Bore, stroke: 77 mm by 58.8 mm.
Displacement: 3286 cc.
Cylinder block: Light alloy, forced-in liners.
Cylinder heads: Two, light alloy, hemispherical chambers.
Valves: Two per cylinder, double coil springs.
Valve actuation: Two overhead camshafts per bank, chain.
Pistons: Light alloy.
Crankshaft: Running in seven thin-wall bearings.
Lubrication: Geared pump.
Electrical system: Twin distributors, one spark plug per cylinder.
Compression ratio: 9.2 to1.
Carburetion: Six downdraft, twin-choke Weber 40 DNC 9.
Power: 330 hp at 8000 rpm.*

Drive train

Transmission: In unit with differential, all-synchromesh, five-speed.
Clutch: Single dry-plate.
Final drive: Closed driveshaft, torque tube

Chassis

Wheelbase: 2400 mm.
Frame: Welded tubular steel.
Front suspension: Independent, unequal-length A-arms, coil springs, telescopic shocks.
Rear suspension: Independent, unequal-length A-arms, coil springs, telescopic shocks.
Steering: Worm and roller.
Brakes: Four-wheel discs.
Wheels: 14-inch, Borrani wire, center-lock, knock-off.
Tires: 205x14 all around.

General

Styling: Pininfarina.
Coachbuilder: Scaglietti.
Number produced: 10.
Period produced: January 1967 to January 1968.
Dimensions: Overall length, 173.5 inches, width 68 inches, height 49 inches.
Weight: 2718 pounds.*
Fuel tank capacity: 25 gallons.
Fuel consumption: 13 mpg.
Zero to 60 mph: 6.7 seconds.*
Top speed: 159 mph.*
Bottom line: $14,400.

*Pertains to aluminum-bodied Sebring competitor.

1969/365 GTS/4 Daytona Spyder

Engine

Designer: Aurelio Lampredi, developed by Mauro Forghieri.
Configuration: Sixty degree, V-12, water-cooled.
Bore, stroke: 81 mm by 71 mm.
Displacement: 4390 cc.
Cylinder block: Light alloy.
Cylinder heads: Two, light alloy, hemispherical chambers.
Valves: Two per cylinder.
Valve actuation: Two overhead camshafts per bank, chain.
Pistons: Light alloy.
Crankshaft: Running in seven thin-wall bearings.
Lubrication: Dry sump.
Electrical system: Dual Marelli distributors, one spark plug per cylinder.
Compression ratio: 9.3 to 1.
Carburetion: Six downdraft, twin-choke Weber 40 DCN 20.
Power: 352 hp at 7500 rpm.

Drive train

Transmission: Rear-mounted in unit with differential, five-speed, all-synchromesh.
Clutch: Single dry plate.
Final drive: Closed driveshaft, torque tube.

Chassis

Wheelbase: 2400 mm.
Frame: Welded steel tubes.
Front suspension: Independent, unequal-length A-arms, coil springs, telescopic shocks.
Rear suspension: Independent, unequal-length A-arms, coil springs, telescopic shocks.
Steering: Worm and roller.
Brakes: Four-wheel discs.
Wheels: 15-inch, Borrani wire, center-lock, knock-off.
Tires: 200/70VR-15 all around.

General

Styling: Pininfarina.
Coachbuilder: Scaglietti.
Number produced: 124.
Period built: Prototype, fall 1969, production version, spring, 1971 to summer 1973.
Dimensions: Overall length, 169 inches, width 72.5 inches, height 48 inches.
Weight: About 3600 pounds.
Fuel tank capacity: 26 gallons.
Fuel consumtion: 10 mpg.
Zero to 100 mph: 18.3 seconds.
Top speed: About 170 mph.
Bottom line: $25,810.

INDEX

Ferrari, Enzo...

ACKNOWLEDGEMENTS

Last, But Not Least...

The author wishes to extend his appreciation to the following individuals in recognition of their most valuable contribution to this book .

First on the roster, two Ferrari historians on whose expertise the author relied repeatedly and extensively: Gerald Roush, the publisher of Ferrari Market Letter, Stone Mountain, Georgia, and Jonathan Thompson, of Newport Beach, California. Another four well-connected Ferrari historians provided important leads and opened doors which otherwise would have remained closed: Dean Bachelor, Woodland Hills, California; Robert Devlin, San Francisco; Stanley Nowak, New York; and Marcel Massini, of Basel, Switzerland.

The historic photographs came from three major sources: The Bettman Archives, in New York City; Road & Track (with the special assistance of librarian Otis Meyer); and the collections of Gerald Roush.

The color photographs are by the author, who used Kodak Ectachrome Professional Plus 100 film, which was run through a Mamiya RZ 67 camera. Two lenses were mostly at work, a 110 mm normal, and a 250 mm telephoto. Laboratory services were performed by Newell Colour of San Franciso, and by Custom Color, Glendale.

In addition to the car owners, named (in the contents section) and anonymous, the author also wishes to thank the following: Everett Adams, Reno, Nevada; Don Andrews, Fort Lauderdale, Florida; Dave Barnett, Springfield Illinois; Ron Barnes, Montauk, Long Island; Raymond Golomb, Springfield, Illinois; Frank Kehr, Ronkonkoma New York; Clara Kerns, Novato, California; Walter Malmstrom, New York City; Marshall Mathews, Woodside, California; David McCarthy, Corte Madera, California; Denise McCluggage, Santa Fe, New Mexico; Steve Tillack, Harbor City, California; Eric and Ottmar Pichler, Gstaad, Switzerland; Thomas Wenner, Lausanne, Switzerland.

In addition to the portion of the author's work that depended on primary research, for his secondary sources, works of the following authors were found of value: Carrozzeria Italiana, by Angelo Tito Anselmi; Cars in Profile No 1, by Paul Frere; Enzo Ferrari, Fifty years of Motoring, by Piero Casucci; Fantastic Ferraris, by Antoine Prunet; The Le Mans 24-Hour Race, by Christian Moity; Ferrari, by Hans Tanner; Ferrari Cabriolets and Spyders, by Jonathan Thompson; Ferrari, The Early Spyders and Competition Roadsters, by Dean Bachelor; The Ferrari Legend: The Road Cars, by Antoine Prunet; Ferrari Testa Rossa, by Joel Finn; Ferrari Tipo 166 by Angelo Tito Anselmi; The Ferrari V-12 Sports Cars 1946–56, by Anthony Pritchard; Ferrari, The Sports and Grand Turismo Cars, by Warren Fitzgerald, Richard Merrit, and Jonathan Thompson; and The Spyder California, by George M. Carrick.

Color separation, printing and binding was done by Book Builders, Hong Kong.

Finally—last but not least—the author wishes to thank Tom Toldrian, President of Top Ten Publishing Corporation, without whose vision, support and resources, this book would not have been done.

THE TOP TEN

1 2 3 4 5

6 7 8 9 10